MY SHREDDED LIFESTYLE

MYPROTEIN

MY SHREDDED LIFESTYLE

Merijn Schoeber

www.myshreddedlifestyle.com

 @myshreddedlifestyle

 /myshreddedlifestyle

Share your results on social media using #MYSL

Publisher: 365Publisherz
Authors: Merijn Schoeber, Sander Roex and Rowan van der Voort
Final editing: Tina Gosravani
Translation: Olaf Nijssen (Nijssen Taal)
Design: Sander Roex
Photos: Nabil El Hamdaoui, Sander Roex, Jeroen de Beer (cover photo)
First edition: September 2017

www.myshreddedlifestyle.com

ISBN: 978-94-92745-01-9
NUR: 443

CONTENT

INTRODUCTION

In this chapter, you will gain insight into why this book is really meant for you (or why it is not). I will also give you an understanding of how to best use this book.

IS THIS BOOK MEANT FOR YOU?

Dear reader, you probably already know me from my YouTube channel or my website Student Aesthetics. Most likely, I do not know you yet. That is why I composed some notes, which may describe you in part:

- You are currently looking for a way to get the ideal body, but you do not really know how to achieve this.
- You have been exercising for several years, but you do not manage to get really shredded.
- You have high muscle mass but are still unable to make your abs ('six-pack') visible.
- Your current fat percentage is too high and you are looking for a way to lower this.
- You currently have a lifestyle and/or diet you are unhappy with.
- You are currently losing body fat, but you have not been able to achieve your goals.
- You have already been on several diets, but you have not been able to maintain them for a long time.
- You want to improve your health but do not know where to start.
- You have a busy life and it is hard to stick to a healthy diet.
- You are a fitness or sports instructor and you want to help your clients with a better lifestyle.

This book is not suitable for you if you:

- Are not willing to change your current lifestyle.
- Believe that reaching a Dream Physique is easy.
- Think that just reading this book will make you lose 20 pounds of fat every week.
- Are unwilling to learn new things.
- Have no confidence in science.
- Only believe what the media tell you.
- Do not want to live a healthy life.

WHAT IS THIS BOOK ABOUT, AND WHAT NOT?

A lifestyle is nothing than a certain way of life. In this book, I will tell you how I have changed my way of life over the past few years and how I learned to build a healthy and sporty lifestyle.

If you read the title, you probably think this book will only show you how to get and possibly stay shredded. Don't panic, because this is not the case! In this book, I will teach you a lot more. I'm not going to teach you what you need to do every minute of the day. In the end, it is about the overall picture. Therefore, I will teach you how to adjust your current lifestyle to stay healthy, but also how to get a beautiful body and even how to increase your life expectancy. The focus of this book is on adjusting your diet and mindset, all based on science and personal experiences.

The mistake many people make is that they often start a whole new lifestyle, but do not have the stamina for it. The most well-known term for a lifestyle people cannot keep up long enough is 'diet'. Many people often start a diet to see quick results, but these results are often short-lived. This is because such diets cannot be sustained in the long run as they are contrary to our nature or pose too many restrictions. With My Shredded Lifestyle, I will help you to achieve and maintain results in the long run. This book explains multiple methods to help you develop your own My Shredded Lifestyle and achieve guaranteed results. An additional advantage is that everything is based on science and practical experience.

HOW TO USE THIS BOOK?

In your hands is the book My Shredded Lifestyle. We regularly use the acronym MYSL. This book is not just a book. It is a book with real substance. There are already many people who apply the lifestyle, as described in this book, who also use the hashtag #MYSL on social media. Several useful extras are linked to this book, such as:

- A website with many useful tools.
- An opportunity to create your own account on the website and gain access to a lot of bonus material.
- An offer of much up-to-date content on the website.
- Its own (private) Facebook group, where you can discuss #MYSL with others.
- Some chapters have My Shredded Lifestyle assignments that help you apply the lifestyle to your life and body.
- A complete step-by-step plan to get your own shredded body.

- The opportunity to share your passion for this lifestyle and even earn money (through this book's website).

In some chapters, there are assignments. I recommend that you do these to get the best possible result. By carrying out these assignments, you can translate the theory from this book into practice. Everything in this book is written in such a way that this lifestyle can be maintained in the long run.

All chapters in this book can also be read separately. If you already have a sound nutritional foundation, I can imagine you no longer have to read chapter 1 (the basic principles of diets). You are completely free in this and you are committed to nothing. This book is written for anyone interested in a healthy lifestyle. From man to woman and from starting to experienced athlete.

I myself have experienced that sharing motivation and knowledge with other 'kin' is a great help in achieving my successes and results. This is why we created the hashtag #MYSL. Through this hashtag, you can share your photos with others through social media. This allows you to motivate or inspire others. You can also use this hashtag when asking questions. By building a large My Shredded Lifestyle community, we can help each share other's stories and knowledge. We can help, motivate and inspire each other. Therefore, I invite you to share the whole of this lifestyle with the community by using the hashtag #MYSL.

MOTIVATION

“ Now it is time for me to share with the world everything I learned from my own mistakes

WHY DID I WROTE THIS BOOK?

The reason I wrote this book is because I fully support this lifestyle. For me it really is a lifestyle, not just a method or a tool. When I had just started working out, it took me a lot of effort to achieve results. In the beginning, I had insufficient knowledge about training and nutrition. Magazines, staff trainers, sports gurus; Everyone had a different approach and everyone had a different opinion. Because of this, I no longer knew what to believe and not. At one point, I was starting to feel completely lost. I have tried almost every approach and method in the past 6 years. It took me a lot of time and effort. But I do not see this as wasted time. Looking at the results I achieved, a lot of the time may seem 'wasted', but if you look at the learning moments from these mistakes you can see how it was not. Everything I learned from these mistakes contributes to what I am now. Now it is time for me to share with the world everything I learned from these mistakes. I want to help as many people as possible to avoid this stage of trial and error. I know how frustrating this is: you are doing your best in the gym and you are on a diet, but there are no visible results - or at least not the results you were hoping for.

My Shredded Lifestyle is a way of life that I have discovered and further optimized in small increments in the past years. I can now proudly say that this is not only the most effective approach to weight loss and muscle retention/build-up, but also the most pleasant way. You do not have to eliminate every aspect of your life to follow this lifestyle. You can make training and diets a part of this, without becoming stressed out about the occasional dinner with friends or family.

For me, it all began with a ‚hardcore lifestyle' in which I was very strict. I was eating six meals of dry chicken and rice a day, I went to the gym every day and I stopped drinking alcohol. When going to a party, I brought my own bowl of food. Do you know what the weird thing is? I was achieving less than I am now. The reason for this is that I often went 'off track'. Taking one bite of something sweet caused a extreme binge and I lost control over myself. In addition, mentally I was not feeling too well anymore. I tried to avoid any social activity as it would 'screw up' my diet. Even if I could not avoid going out to eat only once, I was instantly stressed out. It made me feel like I had been training and watching my diet for nothing all week. This negative energy is bad for your body and you will even recover less quickly. In addition, it is really not a good way of life. At least not in the long run.

I realised building up muscle mass and losing fat is a slow process. Getting my Dream Physique would take years. Then I realised I had to find a new approach. An approach I could actually sustain the rest of my life. This approach has become My Shredded Lifestyle. This is literally my lifestyle, which I have developed in the past years and which I am still applying. This lifestyle has made me lose weight much easier, and I have been able to get my dream physique. But it also makes sure I can keep this body.

I hope you will have the same results and findings as I had. I can guarantee you will lose fat and gain your Dream Physique if you try out My Shredded Lifestyle and follow all the steps. Many have preceded you and I can proudly say that hundreds, even thousands, of people have achieved great results and currently practice this lifestyle.

1 THE PRINCIPLES OF DIETS

“ Each body has a certain calorie requirement to maintain the body

To explain My Shredded Lifestyle, it is important to know the basic principles of diets. Each body is as unique as a fingerprint. One person loses weight rapidly due to a fast metabolism and another much slower, because of a slow metabolism. What is absolutely certain is that each body requires a certain amount of calories to maintain itself. When this calorie requirement is met, we call this the maintenance stage. In this stage, you will not lose weight, and neither will you gain weight. If you take in more calories than in maintenance stage, you will have a calorie surplus and will gain weight. We speak of a calorie deficit if you take in less calories than during maintenance stage. With a calorie deficit, you are able to lose weight. Before I started exercising and watching my diet, I ate a lot of unhealthy food. I often had a calorie surplus because of this. When I started fitness training and watching my diet, I more often had a calorie deficit. In a relatively short period of time, this calorie deficit enabled me to lose a lot of fat. You can see this in the pictures below.

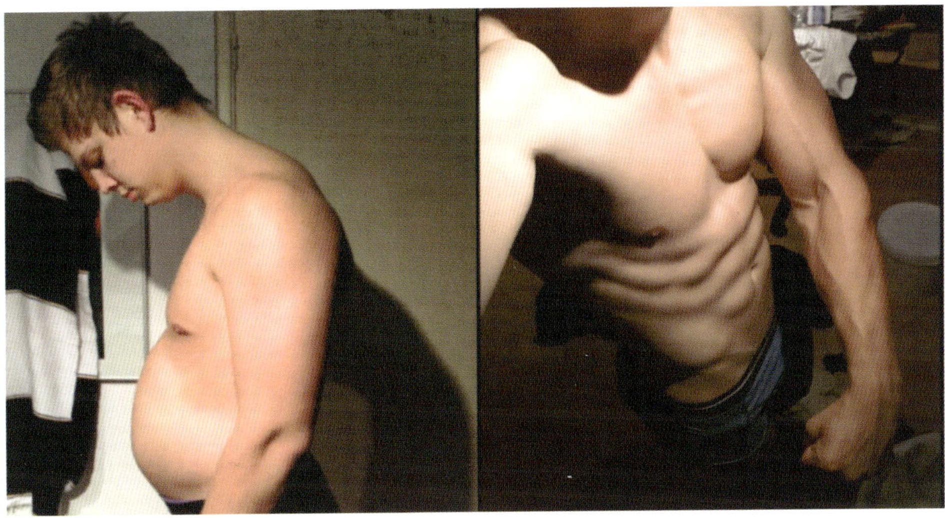

With My Shredded Lifestyle, I will show you in a simple way how to take in less calories without experiencing an annoying feeling of hunger. This, combined with the right nutrition and movement, will make you able to lose fat and get closer to the Dream Physique. In addition, you will feel a lot better, have better concentration and your hormone levels, metabolism and immune system are positively influenced. I will explain these and other advantages in the following chapters of this book.

Now I can hear you thinking: how many calories do I need for my maintenance stage? We will get back to this in the roadmap of chapter 7. Before you start though, it is important to know the background information to My Shredded Lifestyle.

2 INTRODUCTION MYSL

“ Our distant ancestors were not so lucky to have food available at every corner of the street

Now you know the basics of how diets work in practice, My Shredded Lifestyle can be interpreted in a simple way. If you want to burn fat, you need a calorie deficit. This can be done by eating less or by burning more calories than you are taking in. When growing muscle mass, the opposite is true. You need to have a calorie surplus, which means eating more calories than you are burning. You can see this as the guiding principle in my story. The added value of My Shredded Lifestyle is that you can easily get a calorie deficit with intermittent fasting.

INTERMITTENT FASTING

Intermittent fasting means, for example, only taking in calories 8 hours a day of and living the remaining 16 hours on water, coffee and tea. At first this may sound a bit crazy, but it is exactly why I wrote this book. Step by step, My Shredded Lifestyle describes how to apply this lifestyle and why this lifestyle is not crazy but really makes a lot of sense. An additional benefit of this lifestyle is the positive influence of natural hormones in your body. These hormones help you achieve your Dream Physique.

Let me explain this some more ...

Your hormones are an important part of your body. Think of important hormones such as leptin, testosterone and growth hormones. Even if you have a calorie deficit, if these hormone levels are too low you might not be losing more fat rapidly. And even if there is a calorie surplus to start building muscle mass - if your hormone levels are too low you will build it up much slower or not at all.

What I am saying is that hormone values are essential in losing fat. This is also one of the reasons why some athletes and bodybuilders take performance-enhancing drugs (anabolic steroids). These enhancing agents affect the natural hormone system to achieve a desired result faster. I am absolutely not in favour of these agents. What I would like to explain, is how to achieve results in a natural and healthy way. Intermittent fasting allows you to optimize your hormone levels naturally, without using performance enhancers. If your hormone levels are optimized, you will be able to reach your Dream Physique faster. By definition, intermittent fasting is not a diet, but an eating pattern that fits within a particular lifestyle: My Shredded Lifestyle.

By fasting on a regular basis and then eating a lot of food, you are eating your calorie requirement in a shorter period (e.g. 8 hours) in a day. Also, your body will work and react differently during this fast, compared to a slimming diet. It is well known that when you are taking in food, your body processes it into energy. Your body will then use this energy to keep you 'alive' and give you energy for everything you do daily. The unused energy is stored as backup fuel. Your body stores this by turning it into fats. This is one of the main reasons why nowadays the weight of the human body is increasing.

This is partly due to a bad lifestyle. This bad lifestyle can be best explained by going back in time for a moment.

METABOLISM

Let's go back in time ....

The mammalian metabolism has evolved in such a way that fat is stored to survive. This originates with our distant ancestors. Unfortunately, they did not have the luck that food was available at every corner of the street. Neither did they have fridges in their cave, from which they could eat any moment of the day. For our distant ancestors, it was not so easy to get food quickly. Usually their only meal of the day was the catch from the hunt. This catch was eaten at once, because otherwise the food would spoil. As a logical consequence, they gained a lot of energy. This energy was not necessarily needed at the moment. However, exactly this is what the metabolism is adjusted to. As previously mentioned, the body stores an energy surplus in the form of fats. Because the success of a hunt was unpredictable, it was very important to save these fats. More energy was saved than consumed. The stored fat could then be used as a backup fuel. This enabled the body to provide energy at times when there was insufficient nutrition.

For the first time in history, it is possible to get food at any given time. Many people see this as an advantage. For a lot of people, I consider it more of a disadvantage. The disadvantage of getting food easily is that the human body's evolution is not yet adjusted to this. Our metabolism still has strong similarities with our distant ancestors'.

As it is easy to get (unhealthy) foods continuously, this can quickly lead to an energy surplus. As previously mentioned, an energy surplus means that the body will store fat. In addition, we now have lives where we are more frequently sitting down. By moving less, it is harder to address and consume your energy surplus.

It is a fact that with our contemporary lifestyle we store much more fat than our distant ancestors. The difference with our ancestors is that we do not give our bodies a chance to burn these excess fats. This is because we are constantly consuming food and no longer have fasting periods. These fasting periods are important, as they allow your body to absorb fat as a fuel. Today, we are told that you need to eat every 2 hours to keep your metabolism working. The purpose of intermittent fasting is the exact opposite. You no longer need to consume food all day, but choose a part of the day to fast and another part in which you take in food.

In this way, you literally imitate the metabolism of our distant ancestors. With this imitation, you give the body the ability to use the fat it was originally intended for, namely; Consuming fuel for energy during a calorie deficit.

HORMONAL CHANGE

In addition to burning fats, during intermittent fasting the body also undergoes a hormonal change. Here is a small lesson in biology to explain this hormonal change. As you may already know, nutrition contains glucose (mainly from carbohydrates). When we eat, this glucose is transformed into energy but if there is an excess of glucose it is transformed into glycogen. Glycogen is stored in your liver and muscles. The increase in glycogen also increases your body's blood sugar levels.

Then the pancreas produces insulin to regulate blood sugar. The intention is to make the body more sensitive to insulin (but different from diabetes). When the body is sensitive to insulin, food is consumed more effectively. This results not just in a reduction of body fat, but also in the production of more muscle mass. If you combine this with physical exercise, the effect is only increased.

In summary, intermittent fasting provides an insulin-sensitive body with positive effects on your fat-burning and muscle build-up.

It is important to know that insulin is an anabolic hormone. This hormone will cause your cells to grow. Unfortunately, only on a random basis. Thus, both fat and muscle cells can grow thanks to the insulin hormone. With every meal, you give your body an insulin peak. What is good to know is this: During an insulin peak it is impossible to be in fat-burning mode. This is because the body is still in its glucose-burning mode. Therefore, before the fat can be used as a fuel, first the glucose should be consumed. From this, you can draw the conclusion that you want to have as few insulin peaks as possible, to burn more fat.

With intermittent fasting, the glycogen from your muscles and liver is consumed. If you combine this with exercise, glycogen will be spent even faster. This characteristic will increase your insulin sensitivity (a positive thing).

INSULIN RESPONS

So far, you might think this is becoming too theoretical using words and concepts such as glucose, glycogen, hormones, or others. That is why I have visualised three patterns of nutrition to clarify their effect on your insulin response. In the example, three dietary patterns are shown on a daily basis (24 hours). The first diet shows how most people currently take nutrition. As you can see, the average person provides the body with nutrition every two hours. Clearly, even though the insulin peaks are not very high, they are evenly distributed throughout the day. Because of this, the body will only get into fat-burning mode at night. Obviously, this is a pity. What you really want is to be in fat-burning mode as long as possible. Also, these peaks ensure that you keep feeling hungry throughout the day. If you combine this dietary pattern with a calorie deficit, you will notice feeling less saturated after small meals. This is one of the reasons why people are unable to sustain long-term diets. If you are on a diet, you are working on it all day and you often have a craving for 'snacks'.

As just indicated, the average human eats every two hours. There are also people who eat three times a day, breakfast, lunch and dinner. Here you can see how insulin sensitivity is higher and you can spend more time in a fat burning mode. This is because you only eat three meals a day. In this way, it is not possible to stay in fat burning mode for a long time as the eating moments are spread throughout the day and the body still needs to process the glucose before it starts burning fat.

The main goal is to burn as much fat as possible as efficiently as possible. You can do this with My Shredded Lifestyle. With this lifestyle, you eat all the food with the right macronutrients in a short period of time: You only eat during 8 or 6 hours a day. You stay in fat burning mode for a long time, losing fat easily and effectively. Furthermore, this lifestyle has the advantage that you will feel less hungry during the day as there are fewer insulin peaks. During meal times, you can eat bigger meals, so you do not feel like you are on a diet. The last chart shows two meal moments, but basically it does not matter how often you eat during this period. As long as you reach your macronutrient goals and have a sufficiently long period of fasting.

COMMON DIETARY PATTERN

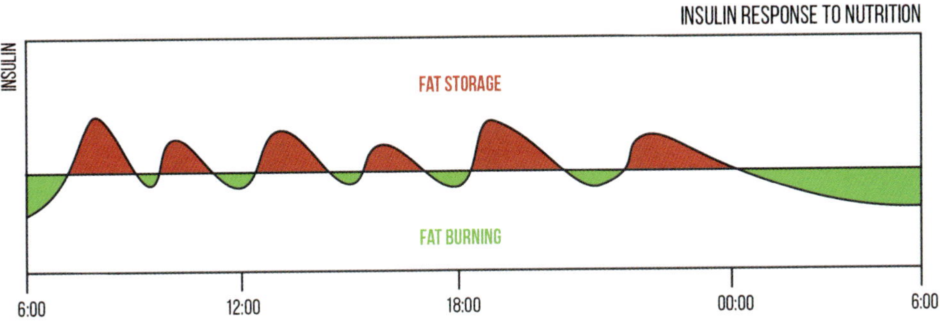

DIETARY PATTERN 3X PER DAY

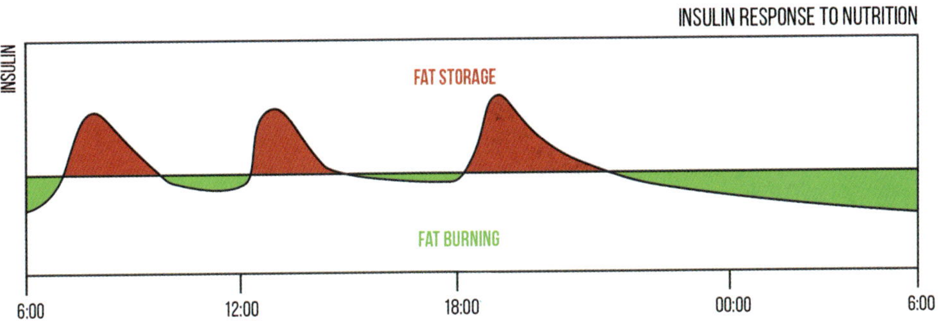

DIETARY PATTERN MY SHREDDED LIFESTYLE

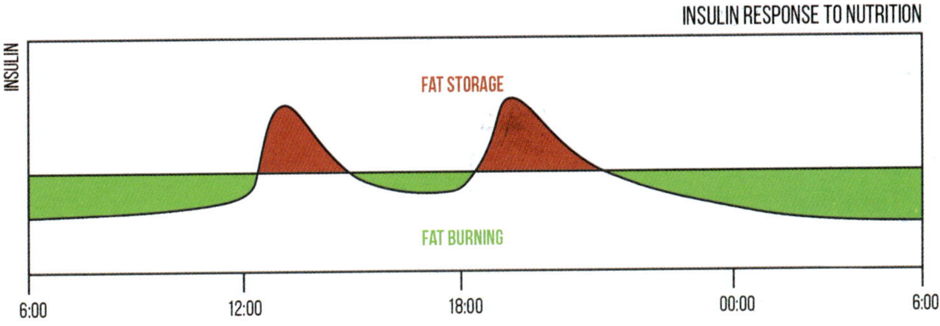

3 APPLYING MYSL

“ Your body needs about 2 to 3 weeks to adapt to the new lifestyle

STIMULATING FAT BURNING

There are various methods available to stimulate fat loss. One of these methods is 'daily fasting'. With daily fasting, you choose a certain part of the day to fast and another part to eat (calorie intake). For My Shredded Lifestyle, I have chosen to apply this method. With this method, I burn the most fat the fastest. This method means you are fasting a large part of the day and take in your full calorie requirement in a smaller amount of time. The periods in which you may and may not eat are as follows:

	MEN	WOMEN
Fasting	16 hours	14 hours
Calorie intake	8 hours	10 hours

The period of fasting seems very long, but keep in mind that sleeping is also fasting. During fasting, the intention is not to take in calories. This allows your body to drain the glycogen reserves. Which will increase your growth hormone and decrease your insulin level. If you eat food after a long period of fasting, it will be digested better and absorbed more effectively.

Again: the greatest advantage of intermittently fasting and taking in calories, is that it makes it easier to get into a calorie deficit. Mentally it is often difficult to take in all the calories in this shorter period.

With My Shredded Lifestyle, it is possible to make your own choice about when to fast, but as sleep is part of the fast, it is easier to choose to start fasting around 10:00 PM and stop fasting at 2:00 PM (for men). For women, I recommend you start fasting around 9:00 PM and stop at around 11:00 AM.

ADJUSTING THE BODY

When you start your daily fast, you will need to keep in mind that the body needs about two to three weeks to adjust to this diet and lifestyle. Once your body gets used to it, it knows it will be fed in the afternoon. You will also notice you have more energy in the morning than before. This is because the body is no longer dependent on glucose to provide energy.

DEALING WITH FEELING HUNGRY

When you start My Shredded Lifestyle, you may feel hungry during fasting, especially during the first few weeks. To satisfy this hungry feeling, you are allowed to consume foods, but there is one condition to this. These foods cannot contain any calories.

If you do take in calories, the fast is interrupted, which is absolutely not desirable to achieve the best possible results. During the intermittent fasting, I always drink a lot of water. This satisfies the hungry feeling and is also healthy.

In addition, I regularly drink coffee while fasting. Usually I drink one or two cups of black coffee in the morning. This just gives me the extra boost for the day. There is scientific proof that coffee is a natural 'hunger killer'. Coffee should be black to maintain zero calories while fasting. Therefore, do not add sugar or milk to your coffee, they contain calories and glucose.

There is scientific proof that caffeine stimulates fat loss. This is how coffee in the morning helps me to realize additional fat loss. If you do not like coffee, tea is a good replacement.

Furthermore, you should drink a lot of water every day. Not only to satisfy your hunger but also to prevent dehydration (especially when drinking coffee). Also, some pre-workouts work well, but I recommend to only use them to a degree, as they do not always contain healthy ingredients. Pre-workouts not only contain natural ingredients. Coffee and tea do. Additionally, some pre-workouts contain calories.

4 OPPORTUNITIES OF MYSL

> Due to hormonal changes, you are able to lose fat as well as build up muscle mass

As explained in previous chapters, fat loss is one of the main benefits of My Shredded lifestyle. Also, hormonal changes enable you to maintain and even grow your muscle mass.

FAT LOSS

The most important rule about losing fat is this: You have to be in a calorie deficit. In other words, you need to burn more calories than you take in. With My Shredded Lifestyle, the fat burning process is stimulated by the hormonal changes of this lifestyle. Therefore, the effect is many times bigger and healthier than for example a crash diet. When following a crash diet there is also a result, but this is just a snapshot. My Shredded Lifestyle is much easier to keep up and it is also healthier than many other diets.

As mentioned earlier, your body will address your glycogen stocks when applying this lifestyle. This will result in burning fat. This fat burning, combined with a zero calorie-intake during fasting, ensures an effective fat burning process. While starting My Shredded Lifestyle you will notice there are times you have lower energy levels. This is mainly because your body is still getting used to this new lifestyle. What helps in getting energy is having a cup of black coffee or a pre-workout. Note that some pre-workouts contain calories. Thus, your fast is slightly interrupted with a pre-workout. An additional benefit of drinking black coffee is that it does not contain any calories and that caffeine stimulates fat burning in a positive sense.

BUILDING AND MAINTAINING MUSCLE MASS

I often get the question whether My Shredded Lifestyle reduces muscle mass or obstructs muscle mass build-up. I have a quick answer to this: "No." When you apply My Shredded Lifestyle as described in this book, I can tell you wholeheartedly that it does not break down or impede the build-up of muscle mass.

When building muscle mass, it is important you have a calorie surplus, so you eat more calories than you burn. Many fitness gurus, bodybuilders or even fitness instructors recommend you to 'bulk up' for a longer time to grow muscle mass. A disadvantage of bulking up is the intake of high amounts of calories. These are often converted to unwanted fat mass.

My Shredded Lifestyle also requires you to have a calorie surplus to build up (a lot of) muscle mass. After fasting you will need to take in more calories than what is needed for the maintenance stage. You can calculate the amount of calories for this maintenance stage in Chapter 7. I understand it feels difficult to find the right kind of nutrition to achieve your goal. Therefore, in Chapter 8 of this book, I have prepared a complete nutrition guide.

This guide helps you determine the nutrition you need to get the best results. Additionally, you lower your fat percentage when following My Shredded Lifestyle. The advantage of this is that contours and muscle definition become more visible. This ensures that the process of fat loss and muscle mass build-up are going hand in hand.

I myself have been using My Shredded Lifestyle for growing muscle mass for several years and it is a great help in having a relatively low fat percentage when gaining weight. I do not recommend this approach for everyone. A lifestyle should suit you and should be sustainable in the long run. The combination of intermittent fasting and building up muscle mass is not meant for everyone. Therefore, you can also choose only to use My Shredded Lifestyle to lose fat. For me, this lifestyle works for both fat loss and muscle mass build-up, but I advise you to see what is best for you.

In chapter 9 of this book I will provide insights into which workouts I use to build up my muscle mass combined with My Shredded Lifestyle. To make things clear, remember that calorie intake remains the most important factor of this lifestyle. If you want to burn a lot of fat quickly, make sure you have a calorie deficit. If you are trying to gain muscle mass, make sure there is a calorie surplus. I hope you have mastered the basics of My Shredded Lifestyle at this point in the book.

5 MYTHS ABOUT MYSL

“ Listen to your own body. Your body always speaks the truth

Regularly, new myths are created to disprove a working method, for every new genius idea or great method. I have listed some of the most common myths and fables. I have provided them with an explanation to invalidate this myth or fable.

Early in our life, we learn that you must absolutely not skip breakfast in a healthy lifestyle. According to many, this is the most important meal of the day.

BREAKFAST IS THE MOST IMPORTANT MEAL OF THE DAY

From reading the previous chapters, you can already deduce that this is not entirely true. When you wake up in the morning, your insulin levels are relatively low (due to fasting in your sleep). For most people, they are only now starting to burn fat. It is a fact that your body is only able to absorb fat as a fuel source after a fast of at least 12 hours. If your insulin levels are low, you want to keep them low as long as possible, because this is when the fat burning really starts to work!

The worst thing to do now is starting the day with a big breakfast full of carbohydrates. This increases your insulin level, which causes glucose to stop the fat burning process. In addition to stopping the fat burning process, the surplus of calories is stored directly as a fat reserve. Now the body burns glucose first instead of fat, which is a waste.

I recommend replacing breakfast with drinking three pints of water. There is a reason for this. After the average night's sleep, your body has had no more hydration for about 8 hours. Your body is actually dehydrated. The hungry feeling in the morning, therefore, is not created by hunger, but is a demand for fluids. In other words, in the morning your body needs fluids more than it needs food. By drinking water immediately when you get up, you satiate your hunger. This is how I can postpone my first meal until 1 or 2 PM. From now on you know they are wrong when someone tells you that you should certainly not miss breakfast.

Another often-heard myth is that you should eat a lot of smaller portions frequently.

EAT MANY SMALL MEALS SPREAD THROUGHOUT THE DAY

A lot of worthless advice is given about nutrition and fitness. For instance, a well-known advice is that we should feed our body every two hours to keep our metabolism level. Additionally, it is regularly told that you should eat every two hours in order not to get your body into 'survival mode'. About survival mode it is often stated that the body would then consume its muscles as a fuel source. These are all fables. Various scientific studies have shown that you will not reach such survival mode before missing nutrients for more than 72 hours.

You can easily fast for 16 hours or even 20 hours a day, if you make sure you get the right nutrients during your eating period. For this, it does not matter if you consume all your calories at once or spread them throughout the day. Your body looks at a whole day's average intake. You only need to ensure you get enough protein in your eating period to build up your muscles.

An often-heard myth about My Shredded Lifestyle and fasting is that it would slow down your metabolism.

INTERMITTENT FASTING SLOWS DOWN YOUR METABOLISM

I can tell you with confidence that this is not true. Some scientific studies show that during fasting (up to 72 hours) your metabolism is not slowed down at all. In fact, your metabolism is even increasing due to the release of catecholamines (epinephrine or adrenaline, norepinephrine and dopamine) and activation of the sympathetic nervous system. The sympathetic nervous system is often seen as the 'fight or flight' system, while the opposite system is the parasympathetic nervous system, i.e. the 'rest and digest' system.

This sympathetic nervous system (fight or flight system) is activated during the day. Looking back at our distant ancestors, you will see they were most active during the daytime. This is why the body has learned to use a fight or flight-system during the daytime. Once the big meal was eaten in the evening, it changed into the rest and digest-system.

The penultimate myth I am discussing in this book is about low blood sugar levels. There are people who claim that My Shredded Lifestyle and intermittent fasting causes low blood sugar levels.

IF I DO NOT EAT, I BECOME HYPOGLYCAEMIC, MY BLOOD SUGAR LEVELS ARE TOO LOW

The penultimate myth I am discussing in this book is about low blood sugar levels. There are people who claim that My Shredded Lifestyle and intermittent fasting causes low blood sugar levels.

The feeling of hypoglycaemia is the feeling you get when blood sugar levels are low. This is in fact the result of constantly eating bad sugars and carbohydrates (a type of glucose addiction). If you eat a lot of carbohydrates with bad sugars, your blood sugar levels increase. Then the insulin will do its job in quickly decreasing these levels. As a result, if you do not eat sugars, you will experience a feeling of low blood sugar, which means that you want to eat again soon.

This creates a vicious circle, making you hungry all day. You are constantly eating and not giving your body any rest. When you start My Shredded Lifestyle or intermittent fasting, your body is not yet used to it and you may experience the symptoms of very low blood sugar levels. In the beginning, you can build up the fasting by letting your body get used to this new lifestyle. This lifestyle is not really new. This lifestyle is in line with how our metabolism is originally meant to function. You can start with 10-hour fasting-periods and slowly build this up to 16 hours for men, and 14 hours for women. If you have diabetes, I advise you not to fast or apply My Shredded Lifestyle. Your system handles substances such as glucose and insulin differently. First consult with your GP and/or dietician before you start fasting.

As you have read, there are a lot of myths about intermittent fasting. Summing up all of them would mean a whole new book by itself. Because I mainly want to emphasize what you do need to do, this is the last myth I will name. This myth is about eating fats. It is often stated that you are not allowed to eat any fat, or just a little, if you want to lose fat. This is not entirely true.

YOU ARE NOT ALLOWED TO EAT MUCH OR ANY FAT TO LOSE FAT

This myth does not consider that fats are essential for a healthy body and your hormone condition. You should keep an eye on what fats you take in. So, it is wise to take in mainly vegetable and natural (unsaturated) fats. In addition, healthy fats are needed for our hormonal functions. In Chapter 8 of this book, I will elaborate on how much and which fats you may take.

HOW TO DEAL WITH THESE MYTHS

I hope that in this chapter I have been able to convince you of the falsehood of some of the myths and fables surrounding fasting and My Shredded Lifestyle. On my path to my dream physique, I have repeatedly found that there are many falsehoods within the world of fitness and nutrition. Often this is because this has been imprinted on us for generations. It is also often influenced by the advertising industry. A good example of this is advertising about margarine. Margarine is sold as a healthy spread with many health benefits, but if you take a closer look at margarine, it contains, among other things, many unsaturated trans fats. This is just the type of fat you do not want in your body.

I also advise you to listen to your own body. Your body often tells the truth better than any particular myth. Another way to deal with myths is to consult literature and scientific research. At first, I also believed a lot of these myths, but deepening my understanding of the science of certain subjects made me come to where I am now. Based on this knowledge, I have prepared My Shredded Lifestyle and I will be happy to help you achieve your goals. Next time you hear one of the myths just mentioned, you will know better.

6 ADVANTAGES OF MYSL

“ My productivity has been a lot higher since I started My Shredded Lifestyle

I hope that by now you are sufficiently convinced of My Shredded Lifestyle. To give you a little more insight into the benefits My Shredded Lifestyle has to offer, I will discuss the scientifically proven benefits in this chapter. I will also give you an insight into the benefits I have experienced in recent years.

SCIENTIFICALLY PROVEN BENEFITS

In this book, you have encountered some of these benefits several times already, but there are many advantages that have not yet been discussed. The biggest advantage that has been named regularly is this: Making it easier to have a calorie deficit and to stimulate fat burning. I have listed some of the scientific benefits I have found:

- Improving metabolism.
- Fasting affects your life expectancy positively.
- Malevolent bacteria in the large intestine are starved by fasting.
- Your body can handle hunger better.
- Brain function is improved.
- May prevent glucose-related cancers.
- May contribute to preventing or getting rid of diabetes.
- May neutralize allergies.
- Improves the human immune system.
- Contributes to a healthier liver function.
- Normalizes blood pressure.
- Gives sufficient rest periods to organs.

There are already many benefits listed here, but there are a lot more. In my opinion, these are the main benefits, the effects of which may be noticeable in a relatively short period.

BENEFITS FROM PERSONAL EXPERIENCE

There are also benefits I personally noticed since I started My Shredded Lifestyle. These may not be scientifically proven or only to a lesser extent, but I personally experienced them. One of the biggest benefits I've noticed is higher productivity during fasting. When I have a lot of work to do, I usually do this when I'm in my fasting period. Combined with a cup of coffee, I am more productive than ever before.

An additional benefit is becoming more aware of your food intake. Only when you start giving the nutrition you take in some serious thought, you see how unhealthy you used to eat. This also contributes to the other advantage I noticed. I get much more satisfaction from 'real' food than I did before. A meal becomes a real (healthy) treat for yourself.

By being more aware of what you eat and maintaining a certain regularity, your eating pattern will also improve. I see this as an advantage, as it is associated with health benefits, but also because it gives me more steadiness. I know exactly when to eat and I do not have to get up earlier in the morning to have my breakfast.

7 ROADMAP MYSL

“ These 7 steps helped me in developing a lifestyle I can sustain

With all the knowledge you have gained in the previous chapters, I can now give you an insight into the seven steps to your own shredded body. A shredded body starts with creating the right mindset. Then we will determine your calorie requirement, your calorie goal and your macros. Next, we will look at the essence of good nutrition, measure your progress and see how to maintain focus.

STEP 1: CREATING THE RIGHT MINDSET

A start is often difficult, so why would it be any different with My Shredded Lifestyle? Before you start this lifestyle, I want to emphasize the importance of creating the right mindset. A good tool is to set up a personal goal. When things are not going as they should for a while, read this goal to motivate yourself or change your mind. I always write down this goal. It always starts with: My goal is to ......

Initially my goal looked like:

> *MY GOAL IS TO GET MY DREAM PHYSIQUE WITH MY SHREDDED LIFESTYLE BEFORE THIS YEAR'S SUMMER HOLIDAY. I WANT TO ACHIEVE THIS BY CONSISTENTLY FOLLOWING MY DIETARY HABITS AND TRAINING 4 TIMES A WEEK.*

When writing this goal, make sure that you formulate it in a 'SMART' way. With SMART, I mean: Specific, Measurable, Acceptable, Realistic and Time-bound. Never write down an unrealistic goal, as this may negatively affect your motivation. Having ambitions is good, but keep them realistic. One way to measure the outcome of your goal is taking a photo of your body every week or every day. At the end date of your goal, compare these photos to see your achieved results. You can share your interim results on social media with anyone who follows My Shredded Lifestyle with the hashtag #MYSL. This allows you to motivate or inspire others.

As an assignment, I ask you to formulate your own goal in the following field:

My goal is to ....

Also attach a picture of the result you want to achieve with this goal. If you are about to deviate from your course during My Shredded Lifestyle, for example by eating candy or cake, look at this goal and this photo. Then you decide if you really want to eat that candy or cake. For me, this technique really helped. It is a very handy method, especially in the initial phase. This is because your body is still in a sort of glucose addiction and is more likely to crave unhealthy food. This method not only works with your goals for your Dream Physique, but also for other (personal) goals. Think of business goals or goals for school.

STEP 2: DETERMINE YOUR CALORIE REQUIREMENT

Now that you have materialised your own goal, it is time to really get started. As shown in this book, your body has a certain calorie requirement. This is also called the maintenance requirement. It is useful to calculate this maintenance requirement. To help you with this, you can calculate your maintenance needs on the website of this book (www.myshreddedlifestyle.com) using the Total Daily Energy Expenditure (TDEE)-calculator. This calculator takes into account various factors that affect your maintenance needs. The calorie requirement that results from this is the amount of calories you can eat without losing or gaining weight. In addition, when building this calculator, I have taken into account other useful data. This way you can look at your BMI and set a personal goal (which helps to achieve or formulate your goal from the previous step). I would advise to calculate your maintenance requirement before reading more. What is useful as well is printing the results from this calculator or completing it in your personal overview on page 49 of this book. This way, you always have your personal information at hand and you know what your current calorie requirements are. It is good to know that this number is completely dependent on your own body and personal activity.

STEP 3: CALORIE TARGET CALCULATION

You have now calculated your TDEE, which is the energy requirement that will keep your body in the same shape. Of course, this is not our goal, we want to lose fat. So now we will deduct 500 calories from this number. This causes our body to have a calorie deficit, so energy will be absorbed from fat stores. As a result, you are really burning fat. Let me elaborate on calculating your calorie goal with an example:

My maintenance requirement	3000 kilocalories	-500 kcal
My daily calorie target	2500 kilocalories	

STEP 4: CALCULATING MACRONUTRIENTS (MACROS)

We have now calculated our daily calorie target. For My Shredded Lifestyle, only counting calories is not enough. We will also count macronutrients. These macronutrients are commonly referred to as 'macros'. There is more explanation about why counting calories is not enough in the nutrition manual of this book. Because macronutrients are important in My Shredded Lifestyle, we are going to calculate them now. We can divide calories into 3 types of macronutrients, namely proteins, fats and carbohydrates. Because this book is written for worldwide use, I have made a distinction between kg and lbs. You can choose the unit you prefer to calculate your macros. We will do this as follows:

MACRONUTRIENT	QUANTITY PER DAY **(KG)**
Protein	2 grams per kg body weight
Fat	20% of daily calorie target
Carbohydrates	Complete the calorie requirement with carbohydrates

MACRONUTRIENT	QUANTITY PER DAY **(LBS)**
Protein	Divide your bodyweight (lbs) with 1.10
Fat	20% of daily calorie target
Carbohydrates	Complete the calorie requirement with carbohydrates

It is useful to know how many calories these macronutrients contain per gram. You can see this in the following overview.

MACRONUTRIENT	CALORIES PER GRAM
Protein	4 kilocalories
Carbohydrates	4 kilocalories
Fat	9 kilocalories

Let me elaborate on calculating your macros with an example: We will do this based on my own weight. This is currently 82 kg (181 lbs). As you can see in step 3, my maintenance requirement is 3000 kcal and my daily calorie target is 2500 kcal.

Protein

It is easy to calculate the required protein. The first overview on this page shows you need 2 grams of protein per kilogram of body weight. If you use lbs, you have to divide your bodyweight (in lbs) by 1.10.

For me this is: *82 kilograms x 2 grams = 164 grams of protein.*
Or in lbs: *181 pounds / 1.10 = 164 grams of protein.*

Fat

For fat, you first calculate the amount of calories you get from fat. Do this by multiplying your daily calorie goal by 0.2 (20%).

For me this is: *2500 x 0.2 = 500 kcal.*

From the diagram above, you can see that fat contains 9 kcal per gram. ***You therefore divide 500 by 9. This is 55.6 grams of fat.*** As we like to keep it simple, you always round this number down. In this example, I need to get 55 grams of fat a day.

Carbohydrates

To calculate the number of carbohydrates we must first calculate all the calories of the other macronutrients.

MACRONUTRIENT	GRAMS		KCAL		
Protein	164 gram	x	4 kcal	=	656 kcal
Fat	55 gram (use a rounded number)	x	9 kcal	=	495 kcal
Total					**1151 kcal**

This gives us a total amount of calories from these macronutrients of 1151 kcal

To calculate the amount of carbohydrates, you should deduct the calories from protein and fat from the total daily calorie target.

This looks like this: *2500 kcal – 1151 kcal = 1349 kcal*

To calculate how many grams of carbohydrates you need, you should divide these 1349 kcal by 4, as carbohydrates contain 4 kilocalories per gram.

1349: 4 = 337 grams of carbohydrates

My total daily macronutrient need from this example is as follows:

MACRONUTRIENT	QUANTITY PER DAY
Protein	164 grams
Fat	55 grams
Carbohydrates	337 grams

For some, this is a lot of mathematics and there will be doubts if the results are correct. To make things easier, I have developed a layout on the website of this book, which makes it easy for you to calculate this macronutrient need. You can find this on ***www.myshreddedlifestyle.com/tools***. I now also advise you to calculate your own macronutrient requirement by hand or mentally, or by using the website's calculator. Also write this information in your personal overview on page 49 of this book.

STEP 5: NUTRITION IS KEY

Success depends largely on your nutrition intake and on which moments you eat. Nutrition has become the 'key' to My Shredded Lifestyle. There are several ways to determine your diet. In this book, I describe the three most common methods. These include counting macronutrients, following a nutrition scheme and eating intuitively (on instinct). As nutrition is an important part of My Shredded Lifestyle, I have written a separate chapter on this subject. This chapter is a complete nutrition guide with all the ins and outs you need to know about nutrition.

STEP 6: MEASURING PROGRESS

Nothing is more fun than getting results. Despite losing fat, it is not always easy to observe it visually. Still, there is a lot happening in your body. Therefore, I advise you to measure your weight every day and possibly take a picture of yourself. The weight data can be tracked in the progress log on page 50. After a while you will start seeing actual results, both in your log and on the photos taken. In the initial stage, you will often see 'fluctuating' values. This is because your body is slowly but surely adjusting to this healthier lifestyle. Another useful way is measuring your weight with a smart scale that can also measure your fat and muscle mass. These data are not always 100% correct, but give an indication. If you always weigh on the same scale at the same time, this can certainly show your progress. The best weighing moment is in the morning, immediately after getting up. First you go to the toilet and then you step on the scales. It is important not to take any fluids yet. If you have such a scale, you can also record this information in the progress log.

STEP 7: STAY FOCUSED

One of the most important things in My Shredded Lifestyle is retaining focus. To achieve this, it is advisable to read your goal from Step 1 every day. This way, your goal automatically becomes a way of life - from your gut instead of an obligation. This makes reaching your target easier. What struck me is that there are always people who tell you you're 'crazy' for eating and living like this. My advice here is to let this go. These people are unaware of what they are saying and often they act from lack of knowledge or out of jealousy. My tip is therefore to be confident of your goal and the way towards it. Because you took the step of purchasing this book and enlighten yourself in the matter, you know better than other people's 'bad' opinions. Self-confidence and determination will help you keep your focus. Especially in the initial phase, I can understand that maintaining focus is not easy. If you are having a hard time with it for a moment, I advise you to let it out at the gym or reread your formulated goal. Make sure you do not constantly get the chance to think of 'bad' food.

As you move on to My Shredded Lifestyle, you will notice that it is getting easier to keep focus and to keep to your diet. This is because it is becoming a lifestyle that is easy to maintain.

Do not just focus on your diet, but also on your workouts. When you focus more on the exercises in the gym, you will be able to train much more effectively and more accurately. This stimulates, for example, the maintenance and build-up of your muscle mass.

If you are going to start My Shredded Lifestyle, I recommend you go through these seven steps. They provide you with a fixed structure, which makes getting the results even easier.

EXPLANATION PERSONAL OVERVIEW + LOG

On the following pages, you can find a format for your personal overview. You can fill this in and check regularly if you cannot remember your personal information regarding this roadmap. Furthermore, after this personal overview, some pages have been set up to use as a progress log. This allows you to track your progress. You can fill in this progress log in several ways. It is, for instance, possible to simply fill in your weight, but you can also log your muscle and fat mass. To do this, you need scales or other tools that can display this data. Furthermore, it is also possible to calculate your weekly average. Here's how to do this:

	SUM		DAYS		OUTCOME
Weight	Mo + Tu + We + Th + Fr + Sa + Su	:	7	=	average
Muscle mass	Mo + Tu + We + Th + Fr + Sa + Su	:	7	=	average
Fat mass	Mo + Tu + We + Th + Fr + Sa + Su	:	7	=	average

It is also possible to measure your progress from the week before (only after the second week). You do this by subtracting the current week from last week. If you have a positive number (+), it means that you have gained weight.

With a negative (-) number, it means that you have lost weight. You would like to have a positive number for muscle mass, and a negative number for fat mass. If you find calculating this too difficult, you can also download the format on this book's website. This allows you to fill in the data on your laptop, smartphone or tablet, and the average is calculated automatically.

PERSONAL OVERVIEW

PARAMETER	VALUE
Length	**cm/ft**
Weight	**kg/lbs**
BMI	
BMR (basal metabolic rate)	(optional)
Maintenance Needs (TDEE)	**kcal**
Daily caloric target (TDEE - 500kcal)	**kcal**

The following schedule is intended for filling in your daily macronutrient needs. You calculated these in Step 4 of the roadmap.

MACRONUTRIENT	QUANTITY PER DAY
Protein	**grams**
Fat	**grams**
Carbohydrates	**grams**

PROGRESS LOG

	VALUE	MONDAY	TUESDAY	WEDNESDAY	THURSDAY
1	Weight				
	Muscle mass				
	Fat mass				
2	Weight				
	Muscle mass				
	Fat mass				
3	Weight				
	Muscle mass				
	Fat mass				
4	Weight				
	Muscle mass				
	Fat mass				

FRIDAY	SATURDAY	SUNDAY	WEEKLY AVARAGE	PROGRESS VERSUS LAST WEEK

PROGRESS LOG

	VALUE	MONDAY	TUESDAY	WEDNESDAY	THURSDAY
5	Weight				
	Muscle mass				
	Fat mass				
6	Weight				
	Muscle mass				
	Fat mass				
7	Weight				
	Muscle mass				
	Fat mass				
8	Weight				
	Muscle mass				
	Fat mass				

FRIDAY	SATURDAY	SUNDAY	WEEKLY AVARAGE	PROGRESS VERSUS LAST WEEK

PROGRESS LOG

	VALUE	MONDAY	TUESDAY	WEDNESDAY	THURSDAY
9	Weight				
	Muscle mass				
	Fat mass				
10	Weight				
	Muscle mass				
	Fat mass				
11	Weight				
	Muscle mass				
	Fat mass				
12	Weight				
	Muscle mass				
	Fat mass				

FRIDAY	SATURDAY	SUNDAY	WEEKLY AVARAGE	PROGRESS VERSUS LAST WEEK

8 NUTRITION MANUAL

“ The right (knowledge about) nutrition is one of the most important components of a shredded body

In this chapter, we have arrived at one of the most important parts of this book, the nutrition manual. With this manual, I will provide you with an overview of all the knowledge you need regarding nutrition. I will also give you concrete examples and tools to help you determine your own diet. To start with, I think we need to study your mentality regarding nutrition and, if necessary, need to adjust it.

MENTALITY REGARDING NUTRITION

In the beginning, your mentality regarding nutrition is important. This mentality is essential to keep up this lifestyle (especially in the beginning). Even if you have in your mind all the knowledge and theory from this book or the internet, or whatever source, you still might not achieve your target. Most likely, this is because you do not know how to apply it in daily life. For this reason, it is important to apply all information from this book consistently and make it a part of your lifestyle and (eating) behaviour.

My approach to nutrition is all about finding the right balance. If you want to be obsessive and perfectionist about everything, you will lose flexibility, and affect your mental health. Then it will be difficult to follow and maintain the lifestyle for a longer period. What will cause even more stress, is what happens when you cannot produce the energy for sustaining the lifestyle. You will slip into a vicious circle and lose all control. First you will start binge eating, a literal feeding frenzy. Then you go back to rigorous and obsessive control, until you lose it again. Creating a lifestyle between these two extremes is something we absolutely want to avoid. As I have mentioned before, we need to ensure there is a balance.

On a regular diet, it is necessary to be disciplined enough and to have enough regularity to achieve the target. Once you deviate from this diet, there is a chance you will regain weight rapidly. Therefore, I advise against this kind of strict diet. Flexible diets, on the other hand, go hand in hand with people who can lose weight, are able to keep it off and stay mentally healthy. This makes it easier to hold on to the lifestyle. That is exactly what you want to achieve.

To give you some more insight into the mentality regarding nutrition, I want to discuss 'following a strict dietary schedule'. From page 75 of this book you will find some dietary schedules for men and women with a certain calorie requirement. These nutritional schedules serve as an example and may therefore be different for each person, as everyone has their unique calorie requirement. Such a nutritional schedule can help you achieve your daily nutrient targets. Personally, I am not a fan of strict meal plans, as they are often misinterpreted. The mindset for many people in such a plan is either "I am adhering to the nutrition schedule" or "I am not adhering to the nutrition schedule". Our minds will see this in black and white terms such as: "I'm adhering to the schedule and did well" or "I'm not adhering to the schedule so I did really badly." It does not have to be this way, but mentally this is what it feels like.

For example, let's take an apple. In your schedule, you should eat an apple at some point during the day, but there is only a banana available. If you adhered strictly to the nutrition schedule, you might feel that everything would be completely ruined if you ate the banana. Mentally, you are giving up and telling yourself you ruined the entire day. Automatically, you choose a worse alternative and eat whatever you want. For example, you eat a big unhealthy takeaway pizza as this day is already ruined (in your mindset). Theoretically, the banana has almost the same nutritional value as the apple, so you could just have eaten it. Your mindset has made you feel that you messed up, so you switch to 'binging'. As previously mentioned, this is a feeding frenzy. I know this from my own experience, but in practice I have observed it in others as well.

I understand why many people like to work with a nutritional schedule. Adhering to these schedules is simple and straightforward. You do not need to learn about the macronutrient profiles of food and you do not have to plan meals yourself. Doing what you are being told is nice for many people and makes them feel safe. However, often this is only short-lived because external factors affect these schedules. A good example of this is that following these schedules is often hampered by holidays, dinner parties or going out. This leads to a mental trap, which means that you do not immediately know how to handle these factors. The schedules will ultimately teach you nothing about flexibility and nutrition. In practice, and from my own experience, these dietary schedules often only work in the short term. Now you have read this, you should not think that diet plans are necessarily bad. Such plans allow you to learn a lot about the nutrition you need to achieve your macronutrient goals. Seeing examples, trying them, and learning how to vary helps you gain knowledge about nutrition and achieve your goals.

Despite all you have read in this nutrition guide so far, I recommend you work with a diet plan. but you should use it as a tool to learn more about nutrition, flexibility, and consistency instead of seeing it as a definitive solution. A handy website that you can use to quickly create a basic nutrition plan is www.EatThisMuch.com. On this website, you can fill in your daily macronutrient target and indicate in how many meals you want to divide this. This website can help generate more ideas for your diet. It is also possible to let me make your personal meal plan. You can do this through this book's website (www.myshreddedlifestyle.com).

Another aspect that affects your mindset is macronutrients. In short, these macronutrients are the proteins, carbohydrates, and fats you eat. How you determine this, has been explained in the roadmap before. Within My Shredded Lifestyle, it is important to eat a certain amount of these macronutrients. The amount depends on the progress you make. The amount you should eat is usually expressed in grams. This is just a number, which you do not have to hold onto too much. I am telling you this to avoid creating the 'all or nothing'-mentality again, which is not desirable to achieve long-term results.

An example: you had to eat 200 grams of carbohydrates, but you ate 210. Because of an 'all or nothing'-mentality, it would lead to eating the aforementioned takeaway pizza. The problem here is the pizza, not the 210 grams of carbohydrates that left you 10 grams over your goal. Because of the pizza, you have exceeded the amount of carbohydrates far beyond 10 grams.

You will need to set up your mindset in a way for you to accept that it is impossible to achieve 100% of your set macronutrient goals. You may have misunderstood a label with nutritional values or have not properly tracked what you have actually eaten. When this happens, it is better to stop at this point of the day and focus on the next day. Like the nutritional schedule, macronutrients are not 'magic'. Do not use black-and-white approaches, but make sure there is a good balance.

INTRODUCTION TO MACRONUTRIENTS

In this book, I have regularly discussed macronutrients, but I have not yet fully explained what these mean and what these mean for you. Macronutrients are nutrients that occur in large quantities in food. Three main nutrients that are essential for humans are distinguished. These nutrients are: carbohydrates, proteins, and fats. Each of these macronutrients supplies your body with energy. This is done in the form of (kilo) calories. The number of calories per gram of a macronutrient has already been indicated in step 3 of the roadmap in chapter 7 (carbohydrates: 4 kcal, protein: 4 kcal and fats: 9 kcal). For example, when you look at a nutrition label, it is reported that there are 10 grams of carbohydrates, but 0 grams of proteins and fats. You now know this food contains 40 kilocalories. Keep in mind that a label often indicates the amount of macronutrients for 100 grams.

You should plan your meals daily using this information. This takes into account a certain amount of protein, carbohydrates, and fat. The quantities of these are tailored to your personal purpose, which can be found in your (completed) personal overview.

IF IT FITS YOUR MACRO'S

Before going on explaining these macronutrients, I want to have a moment about **'If It Fits Your Macros'** (IIFYM). In a way, this means you are doing a flexible diet. I am a big advocate of this way of eating. This method focuses on achieving your daily macronutrient targets and not the type of food you eat to achieve this goal. Many people do not believe this, but I've always used IIFYM in My Shredded Lifestyle and I am convinced it's working.

> *IF YOU CAN ACHIEVE YOUR DAILY MACRONUTRIENT GOALS, IT DOES NOT MATTER WHAT TYPE OF FOOD YOU EAT TO ACHIEVE THIS GOAL. THIS ALSO HAS NO NEGATIVE EFFECT ON YOUR BODY COMPOSITION*

So, it does not matter if you take the carbohydrates from brown rice or candy. You can get your fats from nuts, but also from chocolate. As long as you keep track of your daily goals and not exceed them, you will be able to build muscle mass or lose fat (depending on your goal).

I would like to illustrate this with an example:
Imagine: I need 500 kilocalories. This can be obtained from 40 grams of protein, 40 grams of carbohydrates and 20 grams of fat from a portion of tilapia, brown rice, and olive oil. These macronutrients are equivalent to a pepperoni pizza slice containing 40 grams of protein, 40 grams of carbohydrates and 20 grams of fat.

This may sound strange, especially in the beginning, but it's real. I will explain to you more precisely how this works. Each day, your body consumes a certain amount of energy; this is measured in the number of calories. To lose weight, you should burn more calories than you ingest. Then your fat stores are addressed as a source of energy.

If we are only talking about weight loss (not necessarily fat loss), a calorie can be seen as a calorie, no matter where it comes from. This means that you can lose weight even if you are only eating chips and ice cream, as long as you provide less energy to your body than its basic needs.

Now you may think: "Then why is it called 'If It Fits Your Macros' and not 'If It Fits Your Calories'?"

When losing weight, a calorie is a calorie, but achieving a particular body composition is not just about the calories. To achieve a particular body composition, you preferably want to lose weight in the form of fat while maintaining your muscle mass. This is not just achieved by having an energy deficit. Some factors that play a role are:

- You need to eat enough protein to maintain your muscle mass.
- You need a certain amount of healthy fats each day as they play a major role in hormonal synthesis.
- Your body should get enough carbohydrates for your glycogen supply and to maintain your training intensity.

This implies that counting macronutrients (macros) is superior to counting only calories. This offers you the opportunity to focus on improving your body composition and not just losing or gaining weight.

What you eat to achieve your macronutrient goal does not matter at first when we are talking about body composition. It is a fact that carbohydrates from chips are converted into glucose and glycogen, just like the carbohydrates from brown rice. Also, the protein from a greasy hamburger is the same as it is in a dry chicken breast.

Of course, you should not immediately conclude that you should get all your carbohydrates from chips and all your protein from greasy burgers. Food is much more than just carbohydrates, proteins, and fats. Nutrition is also a source of vitamins and minerals. These vitamins and minerals are often called micronutrients. One problem with candy, other pre-cooked foods and fast food is that they are short of micronutrients. A great advantage of 'healthy' food is that it does provide your body with micronutrients.

For these reasons, I always adhere to the following guidelines. These appear to work well in practice for achieving the right body composition.

- Make sure that at least 80% of your daily calories consist of healthy foods rich in micronutrients.
- Limit the amount of trans fats you eat.
- Consume at least 10-13 grams of fibre for each 1,000 kilocalories you eat.
- Timing your meals is irrelevant. You can eat 8 times a day or 3 times a day (of course, during your eating period) as long as you achieve your daily macronutrient and calorie goals.

The great danger of adjusting your diet is often that people grow tired of eating chicken with vegetables every day. A bite of something sweet can trigger your old 'glucose addiction'. This can result in a binge, which will not contribute positively to achieving your goals.

The best way to fight such a feeding frenzy is to eat healthy foods that you like. I also advise you to add enough variety to your diet so you will not eat the same thing every day. Additionally, you can take precautionary measures by restricting 'unhealthy' snacks in your house or making access to them difficult.

GOOD FOOD VERSUS BAD FOOD

I have already discussed good and bad food, but I would like to give you some more insights into my own vision. Within the world of fitness there is a lot of discussion on this subject. Many people are convinced of an approach that believes in good and bad foods. According to these people, the only way to achieve results is by consuming only healthy foods. It is certainly possible to achieve results this way, but it is very difficult in the long run. In my opinion, this may even lead to a bad relationship with food.

There are few foods that are actively unhealthy to you. There really is no food that causes damage to your body if you only eat it occasionally. The only thing negative that can be associated with, for example, French fries or candy is that they contain no or hardly any micronutrients, fibres, and proteins, but are often high in salt and sugar content.

These calories are often called 'empty calories'. Personally, I think 'bad food' is a better name for them. This term means that this food does contribute to your calorie and macronutrient needs, but little to your intake of micronutrients.

This does not necessarily mean that you should avoid this kind of food. The most important thing you need to be aware of is that these 'empty calories' should not form the bulk of your daily diet. You need to ensure that the majority of your intake is from 'healthy' food (at least 80%). In addition, you can use 'bad food' to increase your flexibility. By allowing yourself to have a diet without restricting yourself, you can achieve a wide variety in nutrition. This makes you feel less limited in your daily life and can lead to long-term success.

VARIOUS EATING METHODS

Not every person is the same on a physical and mental level. Therefore, in this book, I will describe three eating methods you can apply within My Shredded Lifestyle. Before I explain these methods, I want to make it clear that all three methods are shaped by the amount of macronutrients. To be able to eat in a flexible way and still achieve maximum results, you should count macronutrients.

All the food you eat has a certain macronutrient profile (proteins, carbohydrates, and fats). Each food source contains these macronutrients in different amounts. This is not a big deal, if you keep in mind that you need to choose the right kind of food to achieve your macronutrient target. This is why you should measure how much of these macros you eat. In order to determine this, it is necessary to start weighing the food you will eat. This sounds like a lot of work, but you will notice it is easier than it looks. In practice, it turns out you will easily get used to it. Instead of just cutting a chicken fillet and putting it in the pan, from now on you will have to weigh it first. You can note the amount in a log, although that is quite old-fashioned. Nowadays there are various smartphone applications for this. Some well-known applications are: MyFitnessPal (my personal favourite), Lifesum, LiveStrong, MyMacros and CalorieKing.

By entering the nutritional values in these applications, macro- and micronutrients are automatically counted and stored. Please note that many of these applications allow you to set certain goals. Unfortunately, these are often limited or based on traditional, non-effective diets. Therefore, make sure not to use these goals, but keep to the goals you will calculate for yourself in this chapter. I would also like to point out that data entered in these applications is not always correct, as users provide the data. Especially in the beginning I would recommend comparing nutritional values with the values on product labels. This way, you can check if the data from the app is actually correct.

As mentioned earlier, I am in favour of counting your macronutrient intake. This enables me to have a varied eating pattern and also use 'unhealthy' foods in my diet without hindering my goal. Now this is not the way for everyone. For some people this is too extreme, they prefer not to do this. I fully understand this. What works for one person is not practical for another. Therefore, I have described three methods that can be applied within My Shredded Lifestyle.

These methods are:

- **Counting macronutrients;** This is the most accurate method and helps you gain insight into nutrition and its nutritional values.
- **Following a nutritional schedule;** Here you follow some of the plans from this book or a custom plan. You can combine this method with the first method. This can be, for instance, if you want to replace a meal from the plan. With one of the previously mentioned apps, you can then create a replacement meal with the same or similar nutritional values.
- **Intuitive eating;** This is the least accurate form and you will not track your food intake. This method requires sound knowledge of nutrition and nutritional values. I do not recommend this method until you have applied Method 1 or 2 for a while. Methods 1 and 2 give more of a 'feeling' for nutrition.

As you will know by now, I do not like to stick to only a brief description of these methods. I would like to give you more insight into these methods so you have the best possible help in selecting the method best for you.

METHOD 1: COUNTING MACRONUTRIENTS

This first method is also the strictest method. This method usually yields the fastest result. With this method, it is important to weigh all food before eating or drinking. This gives you complete control over the nutrition you take in and often makes it easier to keep it varied. An additional advantage is knowing exactly when to adjust your diet. After a certain period of time, your body becomes accustomed to this calorie deficit. It is therefore important to adjust your diet in order to keep losing fat. By counting macronutrients, it is easy to adjust the diet, as there are clear guidelines. Using this method, you will adjust your nutrition to the calorie goal and macros you calculated. You filled them in in your personal overview (page 49).

The most important thing about this method is that you will adhere to the calculated calories and macronutrient needs. Right now, it is important to have such a mindset that you weigh all food and keep track of it in one of the previously mentioned apps for your smartphone. You should therefore keep track of the extent to which you are achieving your goal. How often or what you eat in a day does not matter at all, as long as you consider that your set (macro) goals are achieved. If you exceed the targets in a day or just do not reach them, you can make up for this the next day by ensuring your average is still ok. Your body does not change on a daily basis, but looks at the averages over a certain period of time. To calculate the averages, you can always use a week.

As for me, I have been using this method for a long time, because I notice it gives me sufficient support. Weighing my nutrition has soon become a habit. I keep track of all my nutrition in the app MyFitnessPal. With this application, it is easy to see the consumed macronutrients. It is also possible with this application to scan the barcodes of food. This makes it easier to keep track.

METHOD 2: FOLLOWING A NUTRITIONAL SCHEDULE

With this method, you follow a nutritional schedule. I have prepared some nutrition plans for both men and women to use here. These are discussed later in this chapter. With this method, I also recommend that you consult your TDEE, which you have already calculated in this book. This way you know how many calories you can eat and still lose weight. It is important that you eat less than your TDEE (maintenance needs), but do not go too far below. If you get too much below your maintenance needs, there is a chance that your muscle mass will decrease. In addition, I recommend considering your macronutrients when following a nutritional schedule. How you can calculate these has been discussed before, in chapter 7 (step 4). The examples of nutrition plans shown later in this chapter are tailored to some fictional goals. If your goals are higher or lower, I advise you to adjust this nutrition plan to your goal. It is easy to do this simply by increasing or decreasing the size of the portions so that you reach your goals. You only have to calculate this once with an app like MyFitnessPal. After that, you can apply the schedule for a longer period of time.

As described earlier in this book, I'm not always in favour of a strict dietary schedule. So, consider the mentality towards nutrition, as I explained earlier. Personally, for me there are periods in which I like to follow a dietary plan. I then apply this method in the following way:

- I follow a diet plan for two weeks, where I eat the same thing every day.
- After two weeks, I change the meal and foods, but keep the same amounts of macronutrients. This schedule will last for two weeks.
- Then I repeat these steps as long as I like to keep to a diet plan.

This way, it gives enough variety while being especially simple and offering convenience. It enables you to do a lot of the same grocery shopping and be profitable (without waste). It is also easy, because you only have to weigh or calculate your diet once a week. This helps you figure out what amounts you need to achieve your goals. You can also prepare and freeze meals for several days (also known as meal prepping). In busy periods, this will save you a lot of time cooking and washing dishes.

Following a nutritional plan can be combined with method 1. With a nutritional app, you can plan meals for a whole week, taking into account your daily macronutrient targets.

METHOD 3: INTUITIVE EATING

As the name of this method indicates, you will be eating intuitively. With this method, you will not track macronutrients or quantities. This is the least accurate method and involves many pitfalls. This does not mean that this method is unattainable for anyone. Not everyone needs to go for the 'optimal' result because, as I said earlier, "consistency is more important than doing everything perfectly".

If you cannot sustain Methods 1 and 2 in your daily life, there is no use to trying them. It is then more likely you will achieve better results with a slightly 'less optimal' approach that you are able to sustain. After all, we want to create a lifestyle and this is only possible if you can handle this daily, without any problems or mental barriers.

If you choose to eat intuitively, I do recommend that you count macronutrients for a few days or follow a diet plan. This gives you an insight into the daily amount of food you need to eat. Then you can choose to use a fixed number of meals a day of approximately the same serving sizes. When you notice that you are not losing any more weight or fat, you can reduce these serving sizes or switch to less meals a day. Then you check if you are losing weight or fat again.

ADJUSTING YOUR DIET

What is important to know is that your body always strives for a balance. This is also called homeostasis. By nature, your body is arranged so it does not want to change, but rather strives for a certain balance (equilibrium). During a period of fat loss, you will therefore notice this to your body. At some point, you will notice that with a certain amount of calorie intake you will not lose fat and/or weight anymore. This is why you have to adjust your eating patterns over time. I will explain how to do this step by step. I have also linked this to the methods mentioned before. Each method requires its own approach.

The first step is important for all methods. This first step is measuring your body weight. You do this every morning on an empty stomach. So, go to the toilet first and do not drink anything before measuring. Track the measuring results neatly in the progress log, which has already been named in this book. Sometimes these numbers may be a deterrent as your weight will not decrease daily.

There are many physical factors that determine your body weight. This includes, for example, body fluids, glycogen, and irregular salt intake. In addition, fat loss is not a linear process, so it may appear that you have not lost fat at all for some days. In order to really measure the result of fat loss, we measure ourselves every day, but we only look at the weekly average. The goal is to lose 0.5 kilograms of fat per week. If your weight remains the same for two weeks, you know you should adjust your diet.

ADJUSTING NUTRITION IN EATING METHOD 1

In the first eating method (counting macronutrients) we will be adjusting macronutrients. Here you can choose to reduce calories from carbohydrates or fats. We will never reduce proteins when adjusting your diet, as they are essential in maintaining muscle mass. Lowering calories from fats is possible, but to a limited extent. This is because you need at least 40 grams of fat a day. It is important to get healthy fats to safeguard hormonal functions. Therefore, lowering the number of carbohydrates is the easiest way to reduce your calories. While adjusting your intake, I recommend not reducing it with more than 100-150 kcal at a time. Generally, you reduce your carbohydrates by 25 to 35 grams or the amount of fat with 10 to 15 grams. A combination of fat and carbohydrates is also possible. Take care that you do not go below 40 grams per day.

ADJUSTING NUTRITION IN EATING METHOD 2

In the second eating method (following a nutritional schedule) we choose to reduce your macronutrients using an application like MyFitnessPal. You will enter your nutrition scheme in this application and reduce the macros as described in eating Method 1 (reduce 100-150 kilocalories from carbohydrates and fats, 25-35 grams of carbohydrates and/or 10-15 grams of fat).

You can also choose to estimate and simply delete a nutrition source. For example, you could reduce a serving by eating one less slice of bread. Then you can check the effect by consulting the pre-existing log.

ADJUSTING NUTRITION IN EATING METHOD 3

With this method, it is advisable to reduce portions spread throughout the day. You can also choose to do this for one meal only. Therefore, be sure to remove a carbohydrate or fat source, but continue to eat your protein sources.

I hope I was able to give a clear picture of which eating methods there are and how to adjust your diet for each method.

REFEED / CHEAT DAYS

At first, a 'refeed' or 'cheat' day may sound a little strange. Also, many people think it only sounds like something fun, instead of something that promotes fat loss. But there is a very important place here for a refeed/cheat day. This is mainly due to your hormones.

Leptin is a hormone in your body. It gives your brain a signal that you are saturated. This hormone regulates hunger and the feeling of saturation. When you reduce leptin levels, the feeling of hunger increases. In addition, low leptin levels also cause your metabolism to slow down. It is generally known that in a calorie deficit, your leptin levels decrease. Because of this fact, you will use a refeed day in My Shredded Lifestyle.

Fats have little effect on your leptin values. Carbohydrates, on the other hand, have the greatest effect on your leptin values. Therefore, I always recommend having a 'refeed day' instead of a 'cheat day'. These terms are often confused. On a cheat day, you can eat anything you want, which of course is a lot of fun. What is less fun, is that the food you consume is often high in fats. This does not allow you to get all the benefits, which a refeed day does. On a refeed day, the focus is on eating a lot of carbohydrates while keeping fats very low.

A refeed day not only gives you the optimal effect in increasing your leptin values, but it also causes your body to store less fat. This is because the carbohydrates will not (or to a lesser amount) be stored as fat during a refeed day, because fat intake is kept low.

This way you will be able to eat more calories because your body stores these carbohydrates directly as glycogen stock and not as body fat/energy reserve. However, with high fat intake, there is a greater chance that some of these carbohydrates will be stored as body fat.

This does not mean that I am against cheat days, but a refeed day is the most effective way to achieve your goals. An additional benefit of a refeed or cheat day is the mental break. This can often be important during a period of fat loss. You determine the approach that suits you best and which you can keep up in the long run.

How often do you need a refeed day?

How often you need a refeed day depends on your body fat percentage. This percentage can be measured in multiple ways. At lower fat ratios, it is important that you measure your fat percentage accurately. I recommend doing this with a skinfold measurement. You can do this yourself or have it done at your gym. The following two summaries indicate how often you need a refeed day, specified by body fat class and gender.

MEN	
> 20 % body fat	1 x per month
15 - 20 % body fat	1 x per 2 weeks
8 - 15 % body fat	1 x per week
< 8 % body fat	2 x per week

WOMEN	
> 30 % body fat	1 x per month
25 - 30 % body fat	1 x per 2 weeks
15 - 25 % body fat	1 x per week
< 15 % body fat	2 x per week

What do I eat on a refeed day?

On a refeed day, you have a different calorie and macronutrient target than on a normal day. I recommend the following:

TARGETS DURING REFEED DAY	
Calories	15% above your TDEE (calculated in step 2, chapter 7)
Protein	1.5 grams per kilogram of body weight
Fat	20 to 40 grams
Carbohydrates	Remaining Calories (Calculate as in Step 4, Chapter 7)

Which food sources can I consume?

During a refeed day, the focus is mainly on carbohydrates. Please note that there are different types of carbohydrates. For example, you want to avoid fructose and sugars, as they affect your leptin values less than other carbohydrates. You can take these carbohydrates, but try to keep these sugars to a minimum. Some food sources that often help me on a refeed day are:

- Cornflakes (unsweetened)
- Oats
- Pasta
- Pancakes
- Waffles
- Rice
- Popcorn
- Potatoes
- Sweet Potatoes
- Bread
- Crackers
- Rice cakes
- Gingerbread
- Fat-free candy (for example Haribo)
- Sorbet Ice

During a refeed day, I recommend continuing to count your macronutrients. If you prefer a cheat day, you can continue to count these too. This way you stay aware of the nutrition and calories you consume. The risk of a cheat day is usually that there are no set limits. One person may eat 3,500 kcal during a cheat day, while someone else easily consumes 8,000 kcal. The person who consumed 8,000 kcal will most likely not lose any fat because they are not in their weekly calorie deficit. So always take care with what you ingest and eat with moderation in the way you have calculated in this chapter.

Personally, I use a combination of planned refeed days and cheat days. For example, if I have a birthday, I will turn it into a cheat day. In such a day, I am still keeping to my intermittent fasting and save most of my calories for the evening. That is how I can cheat a lot and still manage to control my calorie intake.

USE OF ALCOHOL

One question people often ask me is whether you can drink alcohol during My Shredded Lifestyle or while attaining fitness goals. If you look at some fitness gurus and/or personal trainers, this is an absolute no go as alcohol would reduce your performance or results. But ... Like in the rest of this book, I'd rather look at what science says and what I've experienced from personal experience.

I notice that alcohol is often a taboo within the industry and there are few people who admit that they drink alcohol sometimes. Me personally, I am completely transparent here. I regularly drink some alcohol at parties or when I go out. I have found a way that allows me to drink alcohol, while I can still achieve results. Of course, it is not completely 'optimal' to drink alcohol occasionally, but as I mentioned earlier, it's about the thread and how to be able to follow this lifestyle (also in the long run). If alcohol is a part of your current lifestyle, you definitely do not have to give it up during this new lifestyle. The only thing to keep in mind is to adjust your eating pattern on the days you drink alcohol.

As mentioned earlier in this book, there are 3 macronutrients that contain calories, namely proteins, fats, and carbohydrates. In addition to these 3 there is another macronutrient, alcohol. Proteins, fats, and carbohydrates are essential macronutrients that contribute to your body. Alcohol is a macronutrient that contains calories, but it has no (positive) function for your body. It can thus be seen as 'wasted calories'. 1 gram of alcohol contains about 7 calories. You should be aware that these calories count in your daily calorie goal.

My Shredded Lifestyle's main goal is to lose weight, but also to improve the quality of your life. When losing fat, it is important to be in a calorie deficit. If you follow your daily diet as you normally do and will drink alcohol on top of it, you will get a calorie surplus. Our goal when drinking alcohol is to ensure that this will not happen. In order to achieve this, you can count all the calories of all drinks, but I personally do not support this. Alcohol is often drunk at a party or a social event, where you do not feel like constantly balancing your drinks and keeping track in an application.

I therefore recommend the following approach: Use the ‚intermittent fasting' approach, as explained in this book. On the day you drink alcohol, try to stretch out the fasting period. Try to fast a while longer. This leaves you with more calories for the evening. Alcohol contains calories; therefore we should deduct them from another macronutrient. To maintain your muscles, we want to keep protein intake unchanged or even increased a bit on this day. This ensures a saturated feeling. We will reduce fats and carbohydrates on a day with alcohol consumption. We do this to make more room for the calories from the alcohol. The schedule that I use during a day with alcohol looks like this:

- 15:00-16:00: First meal. Eat a portion of protein (chicken, fish, steak, etc.) combined with a lot of vegetables. The combination of protein and vegetables will keep you saturated, making sure you can get through the whole day without feeling hungry.

- Repeat this type of meal (protein and vegetables) for another 2-3 meals before drinking alcohol. For example, this may be by eating example protein-rich food in the form of quark/curd cheese or Skyr. But make sure the food makes you feel well saturated.

- Work out on this day.

- You can eat carbohydrates one time on this day, during the meal after your workout. This depends, therefore, on the time you train that day.

- You now have a large calorie buffer that you can use to drink alcohol without getting a calorie surplus. If you have completely deleted fats/carbohydrates throughout the day (except after the workout), you also create some extra space for your macronutrients. With one person, this will be more than the other, which of course depends on your fat metabolism. Practically speaking, you could still eat some other food or snacks, as you have left enough calories. However, when eating other foods and snacks, you should keep in mind that you do this in moderation.

- After a day of drinking, I recommend that you rest for a day. That is why I always choose to train on a day I will be drinking alcohol. This will help you with this situation the best.

Which alcoholic drinks do I recommend?
If you look at calorie intake, it's important to be aware that you cannot just drink any alcohol. Alcohol on its own contains 7 kcal per gram, but many alcoholic beverages are mixed with sugars and other products that contain a lot of calories and sugars. Therefore, I do not recommend drinking alcoholic beverages, such as beer, wine, and ready-to-drink mixed drinks. If you want to drink a glass of beer or wine in the evening, this is fine and no problem! Hypothetically, this chapter deals with an evening on which you will have quite a lot of drinks. If you want to have more than three drinks, I recommend drinking spirits. Spirits almost always contain pure alcohol.

There is no need to drink these drinks straight, but it is important to mix them with diet soda only (which does not contain any calories) or, for example, with mineral water. A glass of cola contains 85 kilocalories and these will be added to the calories of the alcohol you mix it with. Therefore, always choose a 'zero' or 'diet' version and check the label to check if it really has no calories.

Some drinks I like to take that fit perfectly into My Shredded Lifestyle are:

- Bacardi – Cola Zero
- Bacardi – Cystal Clear
- Captain Morgan – Cola Zero
- Vodka – Soda Water
- Vodka – Crystal Clear

For me and many others, this is the most ideal approach that causes drinking alcohol not have too much of an effect on your fitness goals. As I said before, it's definitely not 'optimal', but you will still be able to get great results. Do this in moderation though. Personally, I drink alcohol twice a month using this approach.

NUTRITION PLANS

I have already mentioned the examples of the nutrition plans a couple of times in the previous chapter. These diet plans are for a specific person with a particular nutritional requirement. Therefore, make sure you always adjust the plan to your needs and goals, as you have calculated in Chapter 7. I have prepared a few examples of nutrition plans for both men and women. In each of these nutrition plans, the total of calories, proteins, fats, and carbohydrates are mentioned for an entire day. There are also suggestions at what time to have the meals. Of course, these times can be adjusted, provided you keep your fasting period.

In this nutrition plan, there are also some recipes. After the listing of the nutrition plans, the recipes explain how to prepare these dishes in a delicious and simple way.

NUTRITION PLANS
MEN
ALPHALETE
ATHLETICS

NUTRITION PLAN MAN 1

GOALS MAN 1	
Calorie Total	2465 kcal
Protein	170 grams
Fat	65 grams
Carbohydrates	300 grams

PRODUCT	QUANTITY	UNIT
MEAL 1 (2 PM)		
Oats	100	grams
Almond milk	300	milliliters
Peanut butter	20	grams
Cocoa powder	5	grams
Stevia	desired quantity	
Blueberries	75	grams
Calories	585	kcal
Protein	18	grams
Fat	25	grams
Carbohydrates	72	grams

MEAL 2 (5 PM)		
Chicken Breast	150	grams
Olive oil	2,5	grams
Penne pasta	100	grams
Green pesto	20	grams
Cherry tomatoes	100	grams
Calories	654	kcal
Protein	47	grams
Fat	18	grams
Carbohydrates	76	grams

MEAL 3 (8 PM)		
Beef steak	140	grams
Potato slices	300	grams
Olive oil	2,5	grams
Mixed vegetables	250	grams
Tomato Ketchup	20	grams
Gingerbread	2	slices
Calories	637	kcal
Protein	44	grams
Fat	9	grams
Carbohydrates	95	grams

MEAL 4 (10 PM)		
Low fat Quark	500	grams
Whey Protein (with water)	20	grams
Banana	1	
Dark Chocolate (>85%)	20	grams
Calories	589	kcal
Protein	61	grams
Fat	13	grams
Carbohydrates	57	grams

NUTRITION PLAN MAN 2

GOALS MAN 2	
Calorie Total	2035 kcal
Protein	160 grams
Fat	55 grams
Carbohydrates	225 grams

PRODUCT	QUANTITY	UNIT
MEAL 1 (2 PM)		
Oats	60	grams
Almond milk	200	milliliters
Peanut butter	20	grams
Cocoa powder	5	grams
Stevia	desired quantity	
Blueberries	75	grams
Calories	445	kcal
Protein	14	grams
Fat	21	grams
Carbohydrates	50	grams

MEAL 2 (5 PM)		
Chicken Breast	150	grams
Olive oil	2,5	grams
Penne pasta	60	grams
Green pesto	15	grams
Cherry tomatoes	100	grams
Calories	499	kcal
Protein	43	grams
Fat	15	grams
Carbohydrates	48	grams

MEAL 3 (8 PM)		
Beef steak	140	grams
Potato slices	300	grams
Olive oil	2,5	grams
Mixed vegetables	250	grams
Tomato Ketchup	20	grams
Gingerbread	1	piece
Calories	502	kcal
Protein	42	grams
Fat	6	grams
Carbohydrates	70	grams

MEAL 4 (10 PM)		
Low fat Quark	500	grams
Whey Protein (with water)	20	grams
Banana	1	
Dark Chocolate (>85%)	20	grams
Calories	589	kcal
Protein	61	grams
Fat	13	grams
Carbohydrates	57	grams

NUTRITION PLANS

WOMEN

NUTRITION PLAN WOMAN 1

GOALS WOMAN 1	
Calorie Total	1665 kcal
Protein	100 grams
Fat	45 grams
Carbohydrates	215 grams

PRODUCT	QUANTITY	UNIT
MEAL 1 (1 PM)		
Oats	60	grams
Almond milk	200	milliliters
Strawberries	100	grams
Cocoa powder	5	grams
Stevia	desired quantity	
Cinnamon	desired quantity	
Egg	1	
Egg whites	2	
Fish oil	1	serving
Multivitamins	1	serving

Vitamin D3	1	serving
Calories	415	kcal
Protein	24	grams
Fat	15	grams
Carbohydrates	46	grams

MEAL 2 (4:30 PM)		
Chicken Breast	100	grams
Olive Oil	2,5	grams
Penne pasta	60	grams
Green pesto	15	grams
Cherry tomatoes	100	grams
Calories	446	kcal
Protein	32	grams
Fat	14	grams
Carbohydrates	48	grams

MEAL 3 (7 PM)		
Apple	1	
Whole wheat sandwich	3	pieces
Chicken slices	3	slices

Avocado	50	grams
Calories	454	kcal
Protein	16	grams
Fat	14	grams
Carbohydrates	66	grams

MEAL 4 (9 PM)		
Sweet Potatoes	200	grams
Chicken Breast	100	grams
Lettuce	1	serving
Cucumber	1	serving
Salad dressing	15	ml
Calories	350	kcal
Protein	28	grams
Fat	2	grams
Carbohydrates	55	grams

NUTRITION PLAN WOMAN 2

GOALS WOMAN 2	
Calorie Total	1345 kcal
Protein	90 grams
Fat	45 grams
Carbohydrates	145 grams

PRODUCT	QUANTITY	UNIT
MEAL 1 (1 PM)		
Oats	60	grams
Almond milk	200	milliliters
Strawberries	100	grams
Cocoa powder	5	grams
Stevia	desired quantity	
Cinnamon	desired quantity	
Egg	1	
Egg whites	3	
Calories	440	kcal
Protein	28	grams
Fat	16	grams
Carbohydrates	46	grams

MEAL 2 (4:30 PM)		
Chicken Breast	175	grams
Olive Oil	2,5	grams
Penne pasta	60	grams
Green pesto	20	grams
Cherry tomatoes	100	grams
Calories	523	kcal
Protein	49	grams
Fat	15	grams
Carbohydrates	48	grams

MEAL 3 (7 PM)		
Apple	1	
Whole wheat sandwich	2	pieces
Chicken slices	2	slices
Avocado	50	grams
Calories	382	kcal
Protein	13	grams
Fat	14	grams
Carbohydrates	51	grams

RECIPES

“ Some examples of ingredients have been identified in the sample plans. These ingredients are great for making delicious meals or dishes. To help you, I have added the recipes of these dishes in this chapter

MYSL OATS

Ingredienten:

- Oats
- Almond milk (unsweetened)
- Frozen blueberries
- (Optional) Strawberries
- Peanut butter
- Cocoa powder
- Stevia (optional)

Preparation:

To prepare these oats, I always mix rolled oats with cocoa powder. This is to avoid getting lumps. Then I add almond milk. I will then stir this into a gruel. Then I heat the oats in the microwave for about 1 minute. The next step is adding peanut butter and frozen blueberries. These will defrost quickly when you stir them into the oats. You can choose to add some stevia. It is not really necessary and is more a matter of taste. These oats are easy to make, healthy and also delicious. If you do not get enough protein in one day, you may add protein powder for some extra protein and taste.

OMELETTE

Ingredients:

- Eggs
- Pepper
- Salt
- Olive oil

Preparation:

This omelette is very simple, but very tasty and healthy. Use the desired amount of eggs, tailored to your goals, and add some pepper. Then you beat the eggs into a fluffy mixture. Heat up a pan and bake the egg with a little olive oil. You can add salt, but do not use too much.

ITALIAN CHICKEN WITH PENNE

Ingredients:

- Penne or another type of pasta
- Chicken Breast
- Green pesto
- Cherry tomatoes
- Olive oil (optional)

Preparation:

This dish is tasty and also simple to prepare. First, fill a pan with water. Boil this water. In the meantime, you can clean the cherry tomatoes. When the water is boiling, you add the penne or other pasta. Then bake the chicken in a different pan using a little olive oil. If you want to remove some fats, or if you like grilled chicken, then you can cook the chicken without olive oil on a grill top. After the pasta has finished cooking, you can drain the water. Then add green pesto and stir the pasta well. Put the pasta on your plate and add the chicken and cherry tomatoes.

Buon Appetito!

MYSL STEAK

Ingredients:

- Beef steak
- Olive oil
- Potato slices
- Assorted wok vegetables
- Tomato Ketchup (optional)
- Pepper (optional)

Preparation:

This meal contains enough protein and carbohydrates and is a wonderful treat for yourself. For this dish, it is best to spread the potato slices on an oven dish or oven plate first and then bake them in the oven at 185 degrees Celsius for 10-12 minutes. Turn then occasionally while baking to get them golden and crisp on both sides. Now that you have the potato slices in the oven, you can bake the wok vegetables in a (wok) pan with a little olive oil. When the wok vegetables and the potato slices are almost done, you can bake the steak. Again, you will use olive oil. The steak can be baked to your personal preference (medium or baked). A little pepper to taste is possible. If you like sauce, I recommend using tomato ketchup. Use a variety that is low in sugars.

CHICKEN SALAD

Ingredients:

- Chicken Breast
- (mixed) lettuce
- Cucumber
- Sweet Potatoes
- Dressing

Preparation:

This salad is a pure indulgence and gives a well-saturated feeling. As a first step, dice the sweet potato into and place it in the oven on a baking tray. Do this at about 165 °C for the first 7-8 minutes. Then bake them at 185 °C for another 3-4 minutes.

In the meantime, you can either cook or grill the chicken. Do this with a little olive oil or baking spray. You can allow the chicken to cool or add it to the lettuce hot. This depends on what you like best.

Put the lettuce in a bowl and mix it with the sliced cucumber. Then add some dressing to taste. Take care you use a healthy dressing without too much sugar or unsaturated fats. Finally add the chicken and sweet potato and enjoy!

CHICKEN AVOCADO SANDWICH

Ingredients:

- Brown or whole wheat bread
- Avocado
- Chicken (or turkey) slices

Preparation:

This is a very healthy dish, and very easy to prepare. You only have to cut the avocado and use the desired amount of it. Then put a slice of cooked chicken on your brown bread and enjoy!

MYSL QUARK

Ingredients:

- Low fat Quark
- Dark Chocolate (minimum 85%)
- Banana
- Protein Powder

Preparation:

First mix the quark with a spoon of protein powder. I like the sweet taste the most (eg. vanilla or banana). After mixing the curd with protein powder, add the banana, along with some dark chocolate. Make sure you match the amount of chocolate and banana to your macro target. Chocolate contains fat and it would be a shame if you exceed your macro goals by using too much chocolate.

9 TRAINING & EXERCISING

> “ It is important to train and exercise enough. It is healthy and helps you achieve your goals

For My Shredded Lifestyle, it is also important that you move and exercise sufficiently. Not only to get or stay in a calorie deficit but also to maintain and increase your muscle mass. For My Shredded Lifestyle, I recommend that you only have your calorie intake after your cardio session or strength training. This is because, after a workout, your body is often better able to absorb nutrients to build up muscle mass and to use it to repair your muscles. What I am actually trying to say is this: plan your workouts in such a way that they are always before a meal.

WORKOUT ADVICE

In this book, I have prepared some workout schedules that can be used for a whole week. After that you can continue to use them. I advise starting with light weights, but as you start feeling stronger, you can increase the weights. First make sure that you are well-trained in the exercise and know how to do it well. A well-practiced exercise is often more important than a higher weight. I have drawn up schedules for exercising 3 times a week or 4 times a week. I also made a distinction for men and women. For beginners, I recommend starting the schedule 3 times a week, as your body needs enough rest periods to recover. Your body can even build more muscle mass with exercising 3 times a week, than 4 times a week. As you make progress, you can choose to start training 4 times a week. This depends on how fast your body is able to recover. The time you do your workouts does not matter if you try to plan them before meals. This way you are best able to burn fat in the most effective way. However, I am trying to convince you of a new lifestyle. I have said it a lot, but you should be able to do it for the long term. It is therefore possible not to consider the time of your workouts and your meal times. It is possible to perform the workouts in a fasting period, but also immediately after a meal. I advise you to look at what works best for you. You will lose fat anyway.

CARDIO ADVICE

As I mentioned earlier, it's important for My Shredded Lifestyle to be in a calorie deficit. Cardio is a good tool to burn additional calories. It is often assumed that cardio burns fat directly and is necessary to lose weight. However, this is not the case. What is the case is that cardio burns calories and can help you get a calorie deficit. You can do as much cardio as you like, but if you still have a calorie surplus you will not lose weight.

Within My Shredded Lifestyle, I recommend that you perform some kind of cardio. In addition to burning calories, cardio has many other health benefits that are also important in this lifestyle. In general, I recommend doing cardio 2 to 5 times a week when you are in the stage of losing fat. However, keep in mind that your cardio is always done after a workout or at least 3 hours before the workout. The time of day does not matter much.

In My Shredded Lifestyle, I always use the following two ways of cardio:

- *High Intensity Interval Training (HIIT)*; This is a way in which cardio exercises are performed in intervals. It is a way of doing cardio with periods of high intensity followed by recovery periods (lower intensity).
- *Low Intensity Steady State (LISS)*; This is a way in which cardio is done with low intensity, but at a constant speed.

You can choose which type of cardio you want to do. A combination is also possible. I advise you to do both once and see which one you like most or feels best. In addition, I recommend doing HIIT cardio a maximum of 3 times a week because this type of cardio is a major strain on your central nervous system, as you are straining yourself a lot. If you do too much HIIT cardio, it can have a negative effect on your recovery, as you are also performing strength training in My Shredded Lifestyle.

High Intensity Interval Training (HIIT)

- 5-minute warm-up (walking)
- Sprint 30 seconds (high intensity)
- Walk 1 minute (recovery period)
- Repeat this 10 times

Low Intensity Steady State (LISS)

- Go on a treadmill and put it on a slope (12-15%).
- Start at 5 km per hour and do this for 25 minutes.
- Each time you do LISS cardio, you can increase the speed. So, you start at 5 km per hour. The next session you use 5.2 km and so on.
- Make sure you can keep it up for 25 minutes. You can also make it longer than 25 minutes if you want to burn more calories.

I recommend starting with minimal cardio (2 times a week) and slowly build this up over time. For example, you use cardio as a secret weapon to keep losing fat while not needing to reduce your calorie intake. If you want to lose weight aggressively, then I recommend starting a lot of cardio immediately.

WORKOUT ROUTINES

In this book, 2 types of workout routines have been prepared, for exercising 3 times a week and for 4 times a week. Also a distinction is made between men and women. If you do not know how a particular exercise is performed, you can easily look up this exercise on YouTube or elsewhere online. Videos can also be found on the website of this book.

WORKOUT ROUTINES
MEN

WORKOUT ROUTINE MAN 3X A WEEK	
Monday (Day 1)	Full body A
Tuesday	rest day
Wednesday (Day 2)	Full body B
Thursday	rest day
Friday (Day 3)	Full body A
Saturday	rest day
Sunday	rest day
Monday	Repeat Full body B

FULL BODY A	Reps	Sets	Rest (min)
Squat	5	5	3
Deadlift	3-5	2	3
Bench press	5	5	3
Overhead press	5	3	3
Chin-ups	8	3	2
Close grip bench press	8	3	2
Rope crunch	10	5	1

FULL BODY B	Reps	Sets	Rest (min)
Squat	10	5	1,5 - 2
Incline bench press	10	5	1,5 - 2
Bent over row	10	5	1,5 - 2
Dumbbell seated overhead press	10	3	1 - 1,5
Tricep Pushdown	15	3	1 - 1,5
Incline dumbbell curls	15	3	1 - 1,5
Hyperextension (with weight plate)	15	3	1
Leg Lifts	15	5	1

WORKOUT ROUTINE MAN 4X A WEEK	
Monday (Day 1)	Push
Tuesday (Day 2)	Pull
Wednesday (Day 3)	Lower body + abs
Thursday	rest day
Friday (Day 4)	Full Body (Power Day)
Saturday	rest day
Sunday	rest day

PUSH **Chest, schoulders, triceps**	**Reps**	**Sets**	**Rest** (min)
Flat dumbbell press	8	5	1,5 - 2
Incline bench press	8 - 12	2	1,5 - 2
Seated dumbbell military press	8 - 12	5	1,5 - 2
Cable fly	10 - 12	3	1,5 - 2
Side raises	8 - 12	3	1,5 - 2
Triceps pushdown	8 - 12	3	1,5 - 2
Overhead rope extension	8 - 12	5	1,5 - 2

PULL **Back, traps, biceps**	**Reps**	**Sets**	**Rest (min)**
Barbell row	8	5	1,5 - 2
Reverse grip pulldown	8 - 12	2	1,5 - 2
Dumbbell row	8 - 12	5	1,5 - 2
Barbell shrugs	10 - 12	3	1,5 - 2
Face pull	8 - 12	3	1,5 - 2
Preacher curl (biceps curl)	8 - 12	3	1,5 - 2
Hammer curl (biceps dumbbell curl)	8 - 12	5	1,5 - 2

LOWER BODY + ABS	**Reps**	**Sets**	**Rest (min)**
Front squat	8	5	1,5 - 2
Lunges (optional with weights)	8 - 12	4	1,5 - 2
Stiff legged deadlift	10 - 12	4	1,5 - 2
Leg extension	10 - 12	4	1,5 - 2
Seated calf raises	20 - 30	6	1 - 2
Weighted knee lifts	10 - 15	5	1 - 2
Weighted crunches	10 - 15	5	1 - 2

FULLBODY POWER DAY	Reps	Sets	Rest (min)
Squat	8	5	3
Deadlift	8 - 12	2	3
Paused bench press (1 sec. on chest)	8 - 12	5	3
Weighted pull up	10 - 12	3	3
Overhead press	8 - 12	3	2
Barbell curl	8 - 12	3	2
Close grip barbell bench press	8 - 12	5	2
Weighted Plank	1 min	3	1

WORKOUT ROUTINES
WOMEN

WORKOUT ROUTINE WOMAN 3X A WEEK	
Monday (Day 1)	Full body A
Tuesday	rest day
Wednesday (Day 2)	Full body B
Thursday	rest day
Friday (Day 3)	Full body A
Saturday	rest day
Sunday	rest day
Monday	Repeat Full body B

FULL BODY A	Reps	Sets	Rest (min)
Squat	5	5	2 - 3
Deadlift	3 - 5	2	2 - 3
Hip thrust	6 - 8	3	2 - 3
Overhead press	5	4	2 - 3
Lat pulldown	6 - 8	4	2 - 3
Bench press	3 - 5	4	2 - 3
Barbell curl	6 - 8	3	1 - 2
Triceps pushdown	6 - 8	3	1 - 2
Cable crunch	10 - 12	5	1 - 1,5

FULL BODY B	Reps	Sets	Rest (min)
Squat	10	4	1,5 - 2
Stiff legged deadlift	10	3	1,5 - 2
Reverse lunges	6 - 8	3	1,5 - 2
Seated overhead dumbbell press	5	3	1,5 - 2
Side raises	6 - 8	2	1,5 - 2
Dumbbell row	3 - 5	4	1,5 - 2
Incline dumbbell press	6 - 8	4	1,5 - 2
Dumbbell skull crusher	6 - 8	3	1 - 2
Hammer Curl	10 - 12	3	1 - 2
Leg raises	10 - 15	5	1 - 1,5

WORKOUT ROUTINE WOMAN 4X A WEEK	
Monday (Day 1)	Lower Body
Tuesday (Day 2)	Upper Body
Wednesday	rest day
Thursday (Day 3)	Lower Body
Friday (Day 4)	Upper Body
Saturday	rest day
Sunday	rest day

LOWER BODY **Day 1**	**Reps**	**Sets**	**Rest** (min)
Hip thrust	5	4	2
Squat	5	3	2
Stiff legged deadlift	6 - 8	4	2
Reverse lunges	6 - 8	3	2
Standing calf raises	8	4	1 - 2
Weighted knee raises	15 - 20	4	1 - 2
Woodchopper (with cable)	15 - 20	4	1 - 2

UPPER BODY **Day 2**	Reps	Sets	Rest (min)
Lat pulldown	6 - 8	4	2
Cable row	6 - 8	3	2
Bench press	6 - 8	3	2
Overhead press	6 - 8	3	2
Cable side raises	8	3	1,5 - 2
Dumbbell skull crusher	8	4	1,5 - 2
Incline dumbbell curl	8	4	1,5 - 2

LOWER BODY **Day 3**	Reps	Sets	Rest (min)
Squat	8 - 10	4	1 - 2
Stiff legged deadlift	10 - 12	3	1 -2
Bulgarian split squat	10 -12	3	1 - 2
Glute-ham raises	12	3	1-2
Cable pull-trough	15	3	1 -2
Seated calf raises	20 - 30	4	1 - 2
Leg raises	10 - 15	4	1 - 2
Machine crunch	10 - 15	4	1 -2

UPPER BODY **Day 4**	**Reps**	**Sets**	**Rest (min)**
Dumbbell row	12	4	1 - 2
Reverse grip pulldown	12	3	1 - 2
Flat dumbbell press	12	4	1 - 2
Seated shoulder press	12	3	1 - 2
Seated side raises	12	3	1 - 2
Reverse dumbbell flyes	12	3	1 - 2
French press (barbell or dumbbell)	12	4	1 - 2
Reverse cable curl	12	4	1,5 - 2

10 RESULTS MYSL

“ Results are something to achieve, so I'd like to share some results from people wo went before you

There are already a lot of People I have convinced of My Shredded Lifestyle. The images they send me from all over the world give me satisfaction. People are happy to share their results with My Shredded Lifestyle. In this chapter, I will show you some images of people who shared their results from My Shredded Lifestyle with me. You can also share your results with us by sending your image(s) to me via social media or by using the hashtag #MYSL.

Lotte Leek, Tilburg (Netherlands)

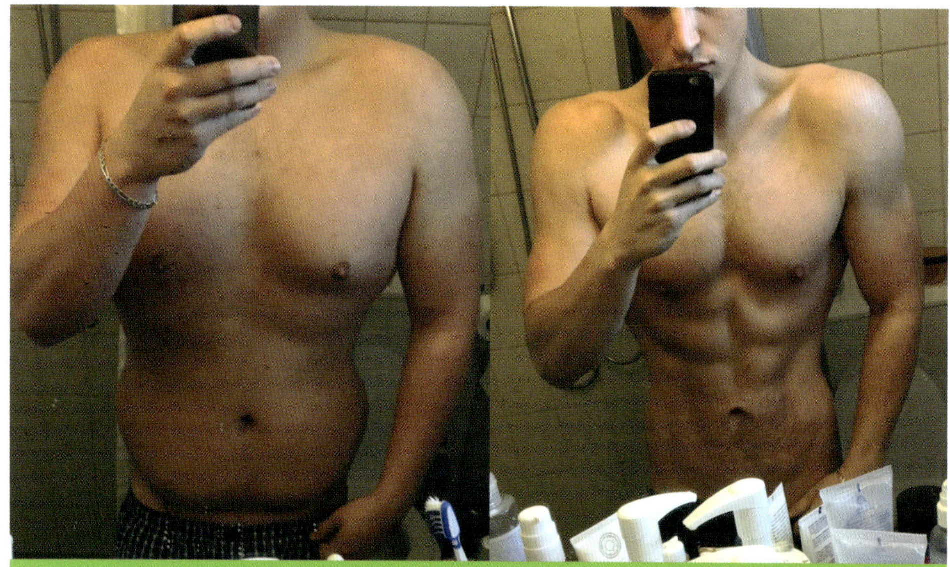

Dyo Morree, Weesp (Netherlands)

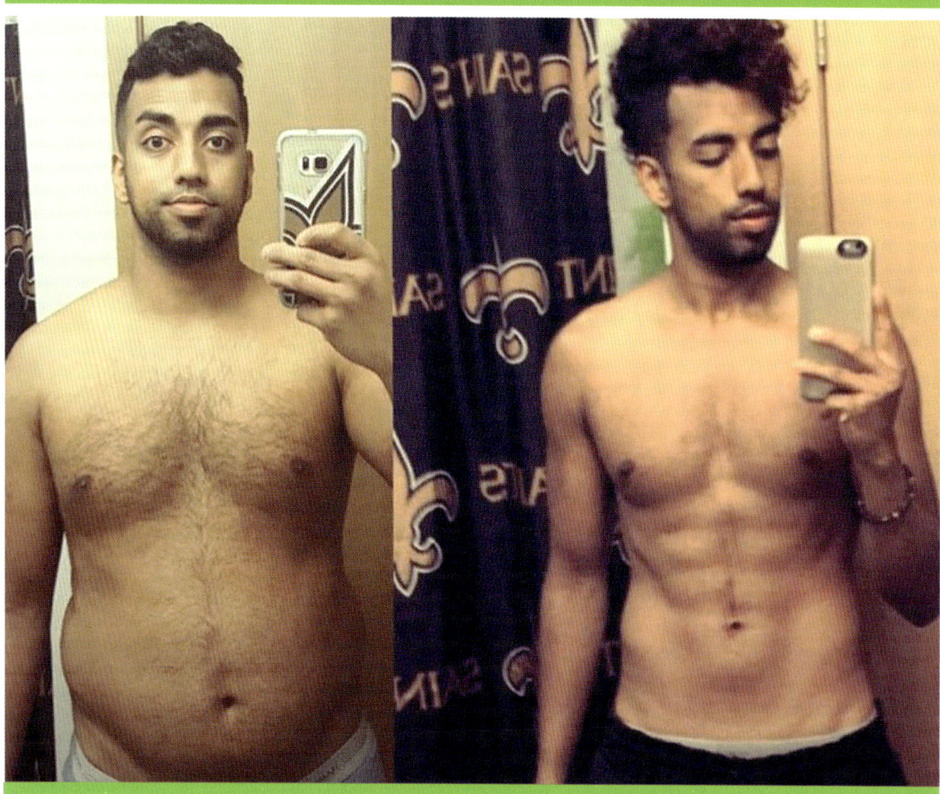

Amar Prasad, Lynnwood (USA)

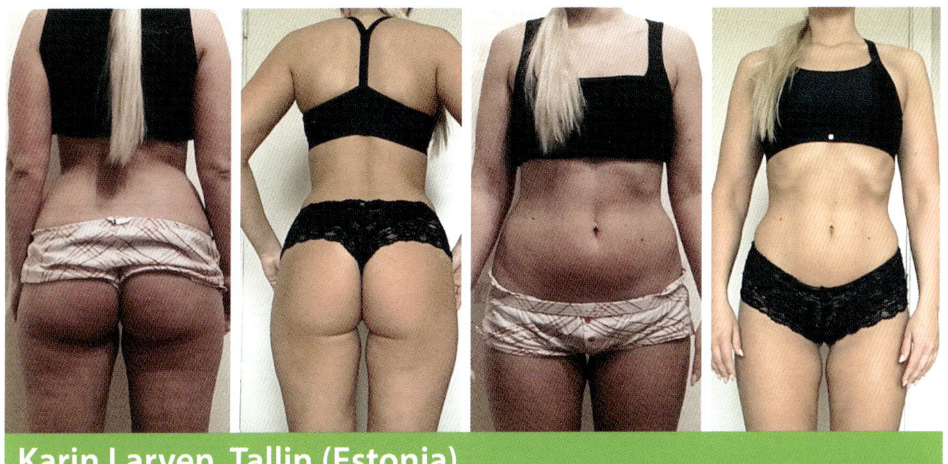

Karin Larven, Tallin (Estonia)

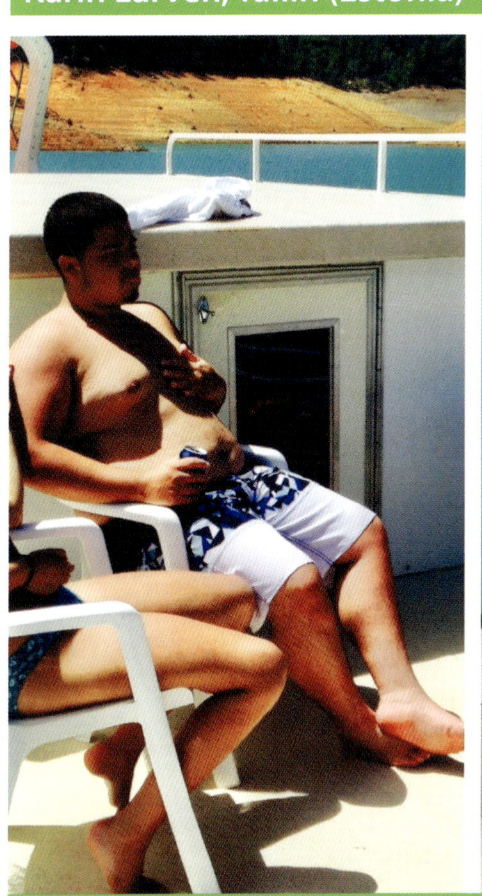

Jonathon Marquez, Oregon (USA)

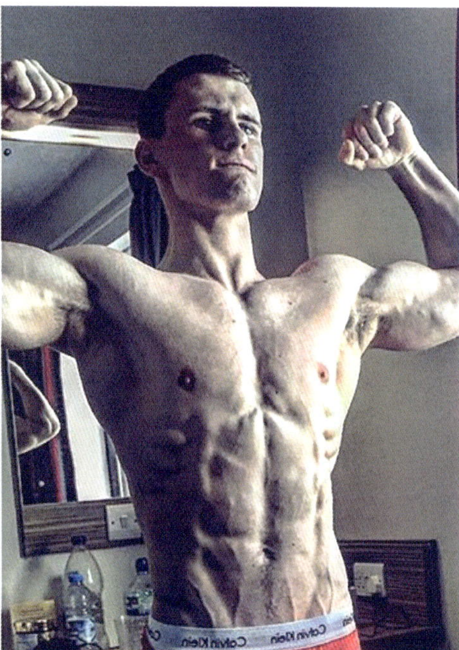

Sam Warren, Glasgow (United Kingdom)

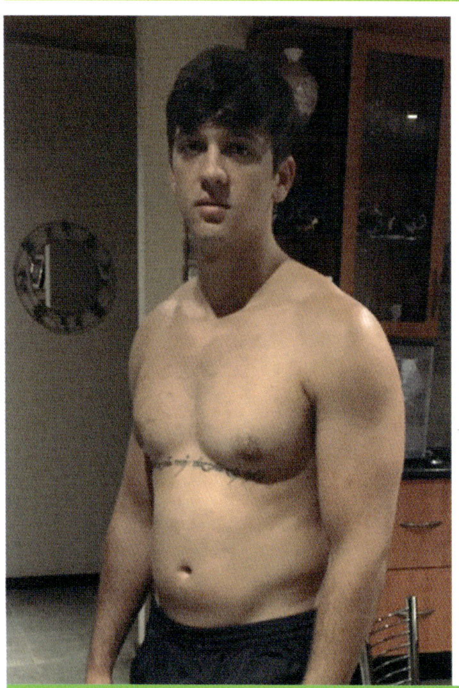

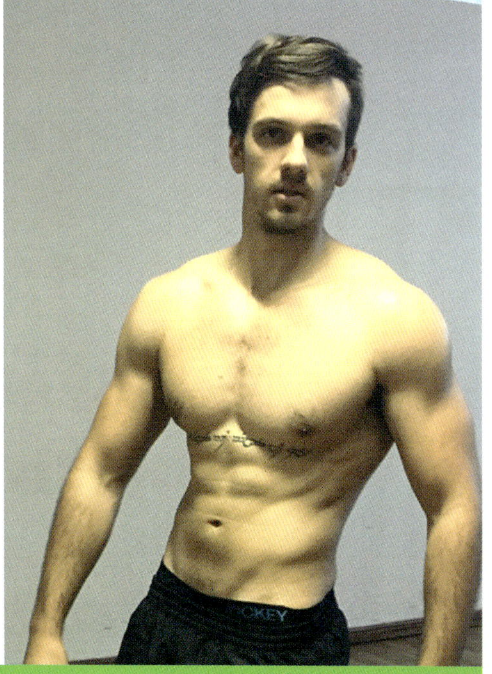

David Giddings, Pretoria (South Africa)

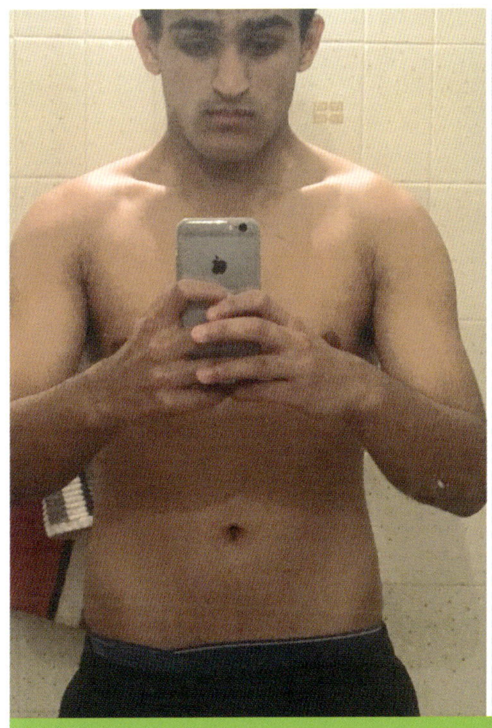

Aman Grewal, Kent (United Kingdom)

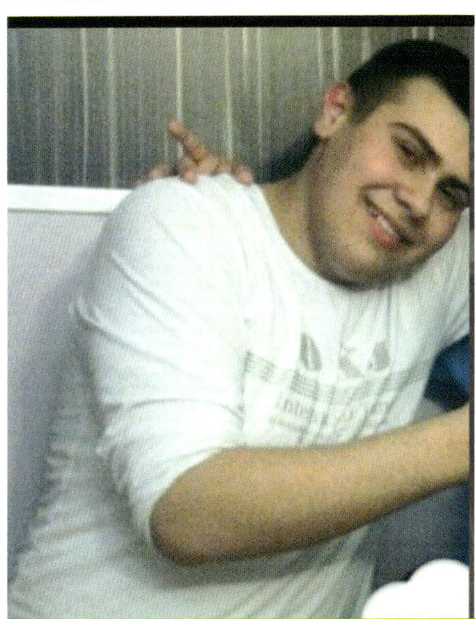

Andrei Rădulescu , Boekarest (Romania)

11 LET'S GET STARTED!

> "There is no right time to get started on anything. Delaying does not help!

We have finally come this far. I hope that I have provided you with sufficient information to get started with My Shredded Lifestyle. I have given you insight into the underlying thought and explained how to apply this lifestyle in practice. I advise you to apply the lifestyle as described in this book. Try to find your own way in it to see what is best for you. The lifestyle has been designed to achieve results, but also to be maintained in the long run. It is therefore important that you look to find yourself in this lifestyle.

I recommend that you study the roadmap from Chapter 7, complete it and go to work with it. Do not delay starting this lifestyle, but just start now. "There is no right time to get started on anything. Delaying does not help!"

Furthermore, I would like to ask you to track your results and share this with all other My Shredded Lifestylers. This is a way to motivate each other, but also to show your results. This will give you a lot of satisfaction and motivation. Use #MYSL regularly to show that you are a part of the My Shredded Lifestyle community. If you still have any questions about this book, you can ask these in the private Facebook group of this book or through the website: ***www.myshreddedlifestyle.com.***

Once again, I would like to emphasize that I feel very proud and honoured to be able to share my lifestyle with you. Thank you for reading this book. I am convinced you can now get started with your own Shredded Lifestyle!

AN OVERVIEW OF ALL THE TOOLS

> “I like helping you, so I will help you with easily finding all the tools needed for My Shredded Lifestyle

There are a number of tools accompanying this book, these are needed to start My Shredded Lifestyle. As a reader, you are free to use them from this book's website. To access these tools you need to create an account (if you haven't already done so). This account makes you a part of the My Shredded Lifestyle community.

To access all the tools, go to:

www.myshreddedlifestyle.com/tools

After creating an account or logging in you will be presented with an overview of all available tools.

ABOUT MERIJN SCHOEBER

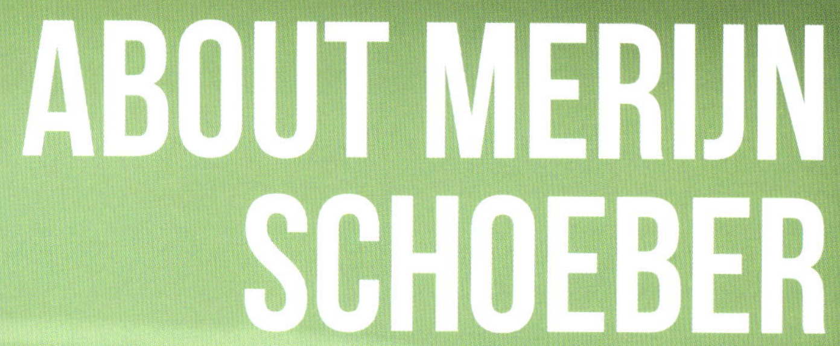

> “Sharing information with others and helping others achieve certain dreams are things I do with a passion

In this chapter there is a brief impression of who I am and what I stand for. I am a self-made entrepreneur with a passion for fitness, nutrition, and this lifestyle. Many know me from my YouTube channel and worldwide online coaching platform 'Student Aesthetics'. I believe that every person can reach their dream physique. By providing information that is feasible and scientifically identifiable, I try to help as many people as possible. I'm not only interested in losing weight or how to get muscle mass but I want to inspire people and help them achieve their dreams.

In college, I found out that my ambitions are in fitness and nutrition, and these ambitions were more important to me than obtaining a degree. So, I decided to quit studying and focus entirely on 'Student Aesthetics'. This gives me much more satisfaction and it has contributed to where I stand now.

I was not born as a fitness enthusiast or an athlete. Believe it or not, but I was addicted to playing video games. I did not care what I ate and I was a big fan of crisps, fast food, and ice cream.

Still, I took the step to start exercising, but soon found out that I did not build up any muscle mass quickly. After that, I started eating healthier yet still did not manage to grow my muscles. Even after reading hundreds of articles and magazines, buying supplements, and following certain schedules, after 2 years I still did not succeed in building up the desired muscle mass.

First, I looked up to fitness models a lot; but I soon found out that these models used steroids. I have set myself the goal of achieving my dream physique as a 'natural'. Through this motivation, I developed my own lifestyle, as described in this book. This lifestyle I called My Shredded Lifestyle. Everything I do, I do in a healthy and thoughtful way. This lifestyle is the result of 6 years of research, trial and error and gaining experience with clients. My main goal is to show the world how fitness can have a positive impact on your life and mindset.

Both in this book and on my YouTube Channel I want to help everyone reach the same goal I did. Sharing information with others and helping others achieve certain dreams are things I do with a passion. Meanwhile, I can proudly say that I helped thousands of people around the world to achieve their fitness goals and have made a positive change in their lives. I hope I can be a source of inspiration for many.

Regards, Merijn

BIBLIOGRAPHY

“ Science tells often more than what others say

Chaouachi, A., Leiper, J. B., Souissi, N., Coutts, A. J., & Chamari, K., ***Effects of Ramadan Intermittent Fasting on Sports Performance and Training: A Review.*** International Journal of Sports Physiology and Performance, 4 (4), 2009, pp. 419–434.

De Bock, K., Derave, W., Eijnde, B.O., Hesselink, M.K., Koninckx, E., Rose, A. J., Schrauwen, P., Bonen, A., Richter, E.A., & Hespel, P., ***Effect of Training in the Fasted State on Metabolic Responses during Exercise with Carbohydrate Intake.*** Journal of Applied Physiology, 104, 2008, pp. 1045–1055.

Dirks, A. J., & Leeuwenburgh, C., ***Caloric Restriction in Humans: Potential Pitfalls and Health Concerns.*** Mechanisms of Ageing and Development, 127 (1), 2006, pp. 1-7.

Febbraio, M. A., Chiu, A., Angus, D. J., Arkinstall, M. J., & Hawley, J. A., ***Effects of Carbohydrate Ingestion before and during Exercise on Glucose Kinetics and Performance.*** Journal of Applied Physiology, 89 (6), 2000, p.p 2220–2226.

Ganley, R. M., ***Emotion and Eating in Obesity: A Review of the Literature.*** International Journal of Eating Disorders, 8 (3), 1989, pp. 343–361.

Halberg, N., Henriksen, M., Soderhamn, N., Stallknecht, B., Ploug, T., Schjerling, P., & Dela, F., ***Effect of Intermittent Fasting and Refeeding on Insulin Action in Healthy Men***. Journal of Applied Physiology, 99, 2005, pp. 2128–2136.

Harvie, M. N., Pegington, M., Mattson, M. P., Frystyk, J.,Dillon, B., Evans, G., Cuzick, J. et al., ***The Effects of Intermittent or Continuous Energy Restriction on Weight Loss and Metabolic Disease Risk Markers: A Randomized Trial in Young Overweight Women.*** International Journal of Obesity, 35 (5), 2011), pp. 714–727.

Hawks, S. R., & Gast, J., ***Weight Loss Management: A Path Lit Darkly.*** Health Education & Behavior, 25 (3), 1998, pp. 371–382.

Heilbronn, L. K., Civitarese, A. E., Bogacka, I., Smith, S. R., Hulver, M., & Ravussin, E., ***Glucose Tolerance and Skeletal Muscle Gene Expression in Response to Alternate Day Fasting.*** Obesity Research, 13 (3), 2005, p.p. 574–581.

Heilbronn, L. K., Smith, S. R., Martin, C. K., Anton, S. D., & Ravussin, E., ***Alternate-Day Fasting in Nonobese Subjects: Effects on Body Weight, Body Composition, and Energy Metabolism.*** The American Journal of Clinical Nutrition 81 (1), 2005, pp. 69–73.

Gavrieli, A., Karfopoulou, E., Kardatou, E., Spyreli, E., Fragopoulou, E., Mantzoros, C. S., & Yannakoulia, M., ***Effect of different amounts of coffee on dietary intake and appetite of normal-weight and overweight/obese individuals.*** Obesity, 21, 2013, pp. 1127–1132.

Halberg, N., Henriksen, M., Soderhamn, N., Stallknecht, B., Ploug, T., Schjerling, P., & Dela, F., ***Effect of Intermittent Fasting and Refeeding on Insulin Action in Healthy Men.*** Journal of Applied Physiology 99, 2005, pp. 2128–2136.

Harvie, M. N., Pegington, M., Mattson, M. P., Frystyk, J., Dillon, B., Evans, G., Cuzick, J. et al., ***The Effects of Intermittent or Continuous Energy Restriction on Weight Loss and Metabolic Disease Risk Markers: A Randomized Trial in Young Overweight Women.*** International Journal of Obesity, 35 (5), 2011, pp. 714–727.

Hawks, S. R., & Gast, J., ***Weight Loss Management: A Path Lit Darkly.*** Health Education & Behavior, 25 (3), 1998, pp. 371–382.

Heilbronn, L. K., Civitarese, A. E., Bogacka, I., Smith, S. R., Hulver, M., & Ravussin, E., ***Glucose Tolerance and Skeletal Muscle Gene Expression in Response to Alternate Day Fasting.*** Obesity Research, 13 (3), 2005, pp. 574–581.

Heilbronn, L. K., Smith, S. R., Martin, C. K., Anton, S. D., & Ravussin, E., ***Alternate-Day Fasting in Nonobese Subjects: Effects on Body Weight, Body Composition, and Energy Metabolism.*** The American Journal of Clinical Nutrition, 81 (1), 2005, pp. 69–73.

Johnson, S., & Leck, K., ***The Effects of Dietary Fasting on Physical Balance among Healthy Young Women.*** Nutrition Journal, 9, 2010, pp. 18.

Johnstone, A. M., ***Fasting - The Ultimate Diet?*** Obesity Reviews, 8 (3), 2007, pp. 211–222.

Jørgensen, J. O., Vahl, N., Dall, R., & Christiansen, J. S., ***Resting metabolic rate in healthy adults: relation to growth hormone status and leptin levels.*** Metabolism, 47 (9), 1998, pp. 1134-1139.

Klok, M. D., Jakobsdottir, S., & Drent, M. L., ***The role of leptin and ghrelin in the regulation of food intake and body weight in humans: a review.*** Obesity Reviews, 8 (1), 2007, pp. 21-34.

Lemon, P. W., & Mullin, J. P., ***Effect of Initial Muscle Glycogen Levels on Protein Catabolism during Exercise.*** Journal of Applied Physiology, 48 (4), 1980, pp. 624–629.

Longo, V. D., & Mattson, M. P., ***Fasting: Molecular Mechanisms and Clinical Applications.*** Cell Metabolism, 19 (2), 2014, pp. 181–192.

Loy, S. F., Conlee, R. K., Winder, W. W., Nelson, A. G., Arnall, D. A., & Fisher, A.G., ***Effects of 24-Hour at Two Different Fast on Cycling Endurance Time Intensities.*** Journal of Applied Physiology, 61 (2), 1986, pp. 654–659.

Perry, C. G. R., Heigenhauser, G. J. F., Bonen, A., & Spriet, L. L., ***High-intensity aerobic interval training increases fat and carbohydrate metabolic capacities in human skeletal muscle.*** Applied Physiology, Nutrition, and Metabolism, 33 (6), 2008, pp.1112-1123.

Romon, M., Lebel, P., Velly, C., Marecaux, N., Fruchart, J. C., & Dallongeville, J., ***Leptin response to carbohydrate or fat meal and association with subsequent satiety and energy intake.*** American Journal of Physiology-Endocrinology And Metabolism, 277 (5), 1999, pp. 855-861.

Schabort, E. J., Bosch, A. N., Weltan, S. M., & Noakes, T. D., T***he Effect of a Preexercise Meal on Time to Fatigue during Prolonged Cycling Exercise.*** Medicine and Science in Sports and Exercise, 31 (3), 1999, pp. 464–471.

Schoenfeld, B., ***Does Cardio after an Overnight Fast Maximize Fat Loss?*** Strength and Conditioning Journal, 33 (1), 2011, pp. 23–25.

Soeters, M. R., Lammers, N. M., Dubbelhuis, P. F., Ackermans, T., Jonkers-Schuitema, C. F., Fliers, E., Sauerwein, H. P., Aerts, J. M., & Serlie, M. J., ***Intermittent Fasting Does Not Affect Whole-Body Glucose, Lipid, or Protein Metabolism.*** American Journal of Clinical Nutrition 2009 (90), 2009, pp. 1244–1251.

Stote, K. S., Baer, D. J., Spears, K., Paul, D. R., Harris, G. K., Rumpler, W. V., Strycula, P. et al. ***A Controlled Trial of Reduced Meal Frequency without Caloric Restriction in Healthy, Normal-Weight, Middle-Aged Adults.*** The American Journal of Clinical Nutrition, 85 (4), 2007, pp. 981–988.

Varady, K. A., ***Intermittent versus Daily Calorie Restriction: Which Diet Regimen Is More Effective for Weight Loss?*** Obesity Reviews, 12 (7), 2011, pp. 593–601.

Varady, K. A., Bhutani, S., Church, E. C., & Klempel, m. C., ***Short-Term Modified Alternate-Day Fasting: A Novel Dietary Strategy for Weight Loss and Cardioprotection in Obese Adults.*** American Journal of Clinical Nutrition, 90, 2009, pp. 1138–1143.

Varnier, M., Sarto, P., Martines, D., Lora, L., Carmignoto, F., Leese, G. P., & Naccarato, R., ***Effect of Infusing Branched-Chain Amino Acid during Incremental Exercise with Reduced Muscle Glycogen Content.*** European Journal of Applied Physiology, 69 (1), 1994, pp. 26–31.

Weigle, D. S., Duell, P. B., Connor, W. E., Steiner, R. A., Soules, M. R., & Kuijper, J. L., ***Effect of Fasting, Refeeding, and Dietary Fat Restriction on Plasma Leptin Levels***. The Journal of Clinical Endocrinology & Metabolism, 82 (2), 1997, pp. 561-565.

Wing, R. R., Marcus, M. D., Blair, E. H., & Burton, L. R., ***Psychological Responses of Obese Type II Diabetic Subjects to Very-Low-Calorie Diet.*** Diabetes Care, 14 (7), 1991, pp. 596–599.

Zwetsloot, K. A., John, C. S., Lawrence, M. M., Battista, R. A., Shanely, R. A., ***High-intensity interval training induces a modest systemic inflammatory respons in active, young men.*** Journal of Inflammation Research, 7 (1), 2014, pp. 9-16